Birmingham

– BEFORE THE –

Electric Tram

*Horse, Steam, Cable and Accumulator Trams
from 1872 until 1911*

DAVID HARVEY

AMBERLEY

FRONT COVER ABOVE: CAR 118

The last cable trams bought by the financially ailing BCT Company were purchased from the Falcon Company in 1895. These double-deck bogie open-top five side-windowed trams were purchased at the time when the only financially successful part of the BCT 'empire' was the Handsworth cable route, a fact which is confirmed by the need to buy them in order to cope with the continued rise in passenger numbers. The tram is largely devoid of advertisements suggesting that it was parked outside the New Inns near to the date of the final closure of the CBT service on 30 June 1911.

FRONT COVER BELOW: LOCO 45 AND TRAILER 63

The Falcon Engine Company locomotive 45 in 1885 pulls double-ended sixty-seat trailer 63, also built by Falcon during the following year, which stands in Alcester Road with the locomotive half reversed out of the coke yard between St Mary's Row and Farquhar Road, when it was being operated by the City of Birmingham Tramways. The steam tram gained a poor reputation, but when properly maintained 'the shufflers', so named because of their shuffling gait as the pistons pumped back and forth, were very efficient movers of people.

First published 2013

Amberley Publishing
The Hill, Stroud
Gloucestershire, GL5 4EP

www.amberley-books.com

Copyright © David Harvey 2013

The right of David Harvey to be identified as the Author
of this work has been asserted in accordance with the
Copyrights, Designs and Patents Act 1988.

British Library Cataloguing in Publication Data.
A catalogue record for this book is available from the British Library.

ISBN 978 1 4456 1622 3
E-book ISBN 978 1 4456 1637 7

Typeset in 10pt on 13pt Sabon.
Typesetting and Origination by Amberley Publishing.
Printed in the UK.

ACKNOWLEDGEMENTS

The author is grateful to the many photographers, acknowledged in the text, whose pictures are found herein. As nearly all these photographs were taken over 100 years ago, there is alas none of those early transport enthusiasts left alive to thank. Where the photographer is known, the photographs are credited accordingly. If there is no credit given, they come from my own collection.

Special thanks are due to my wife Diana for her splendid proofreading, and for letting me off normal domestic duties so that I could spend the wee small hours researching and typing this book. Roger Smith's excellent maps are wonderfully informative and help the reader to place the photographs in their correct location, while David Gladwin tried very hard to unravel some of the contradictory information which had been discovered. The book would not have been possible without the continued encouragement given by Louis Archard and Campbell McCutcheon of Amberley Publishing.

Chronology of Opening and Closing Dates of Steam, Cable, Horse and Accumulator Tram Routes in Birmingham

- Birmingham & Aston Old Square to Witton line opened 26/12/82, closed 13/9/04.
- Birmingham & Aston Old Square to Aston Cross and Salford Bridge line opened 23/2/85, closed 13/11/04.
- BCT Old Square to Perry Barr line opened 25/11/84, closed 31/12/06.
- BCT Moseley via Moseley Road line opened 29/12/84, closed 31/12/06.
- BCT Lozells to Aston Station, Lichfield Road, 1/11/1885, closed 26/10/04.
- BCT Old Square to Nechells via Gosta Green opened 29/3/1885, Nechells section from Bloombury Street closed by 11/1885.
- BCT Old Square to Saltley via Gosta Green line opened 24/11/85 closed 31/12/06.
- BCT Moat Row to Sparkhill opened 11/05/85, extended to Hill Street 20/6/85, closed 31/12/1906.
- BCT Small Heath via Coventry Road opened 16/1/86, closed 22/2/05.
- BCT Moseley via Balsall Heath line opened 19/7/86, extended to Kings Heath 1/2/87, closed 31/12/06.
- BCT Lozells via Wheeler Street line opened 25/10/86, closed 31/12/06.
- BCT Nechells horse line opened 11/11/84, closed 31/12/06.
- BCT Warwick Road line opened 16/11/87, closed '88.
- BCT Monmouth Street to Hockley Brook cable line opened 24/3/88, closed 30/6/11.
- BCT Hockley Brook to New Inns cable line opened 20/4/89, closed 30/6/11.
- BCT Suffolk Street to Bournbrook accumulator line, opened 24/7/90, closed 5/01.
- BCT Stratford Road (St John's Road) to College Road, Springfield, opened 5/5/99, closed 31/12/06.

INTRODUCTION

The difficulty in writing this book has been in attempting to marry up historical information from a variety of sources. Bearing in mind that the most recent events described in the book took place at the latest at the end of 1911 and go back as far as 1873, many of the sources inevitably contradict each other, especially over dates. Even some routes operated by steam trams in Birmingham are difficult to unravel, but without becoming too bogged down in the necessary Board of Trade Regulations of the late nineteenth century, this book has always had as its prime aim to take a pictorial view of tram operation in the pre-electric era. Inevitably, some of the photographs are less than perfect, but all show some aspects of the early mechanical forms of urban transport that were being employed in Birmingham.

A GENERAL HISTORY

The City of Birmingham Tramways Company, and its predecessor the Birmingham Central Tramways Company, was extremely unusual in that it operated horse, steam, cable, accumulator and electric tramcars in the Birmingham area.

On 22 December 1881 Birmingham & Suburban Tramways was incorporated as a limited company and on 24 January 1883 the company name was changed to Birmingham Central Tramway Company Ltd. The new company obtained twenty-one-year leases to operate trams on eight routes over their own tram tracks.

Operation of their first steam tramway in Birmingham commenced on 25 November 1884 to Perry Barr. A completely separate section to Moseley, to the south of Birmingham, opened just over one month later and the company gradually developed a network of horse-, steam-, cable- and accumulator-powered routes across the town. Steam tram routes were built to Lozells, Saltley, Sparkhill, Small Heath, Balsall Heath and Wheeler Street, and were all completed by 1886. The cable trams began operation on 24 March 1888 and the accumulator trams started on 24 July 1890.

Unfortunately BCT was very badly managed, due in part to this mixture of tramway systems, which proved to be disparate, increasingly unprofitable and unsatisfactory. However, the cable operation was always profitable and the steam tram routes, although increasingly unpopular, were generally making money, especially on the Moseley Road, Stratford Road and Perry Barr services. The accumulator route was never totally satisfactory and, although pioneering, its maintenance costs rather outweighed the profits. The fact that the company leased most of its lines and the obvious need to develop overhead electric propulsion proved to be financially divisive. The Corporation's intransigence over allowing the company to develop overhead electric-powered routes proved to be BCT's 'Sword of Damocles'. Thus on 29 September 1896 the assets of the Birmingham Central Tramways Company were acquired by a new company named the

City of Birmingham Tramways Company Ltd, which intended to convert the whole system to overhead electric. It was anticipated that the approval of Birmingham Corporation would be forthcoming; however, negotiations broke down on the 7 June 1898 without agreement, as it was the Corporation's intention to own and build their own municipally owned system.

At the beginning of the twentieth century, the fortunes of CBT seemed to be in the ascendency as they opened the first overhead-powered electric tram route along Bristol Road to Selly Oak from the original battery tram terminus in Suffolk Street on Tuesday 14 May 1901. The Kings Norton and Northfield Urban District Council obtained the necessary powers to build an electric overhead tramway along Pershore Road to Cotteridge in 1901. The route of the new line was linked to the City of Birmingham Tramways Bristol Road route via Pebble Mill Road. As a result of this, the UDC approached the tramway company to work the line to Cotteridge on its behalf.

The Pershore Road service was opened on 20 May 1904 between the stub terminus of the recently abandoned accumulator trams in Suffolk Street and the temporary terminus near Mayfield Road, Stirchley. The line was extended to Cotteridge on 23 June 1904.

But there was a cloud on the horizon that eventually would cause the downfall of the Company. CBT's twenty-one-year lease on the operation of the Bristol Road and Pershore Road routes was due to expire in 1911. The electrification agreement of 21 July 1900 allowed for Birmingham Corporation to purchase all the tram rolling stock, electrical feeders and overhead within the city boundary by 1 July 1911.

The Birmingham & Aston Tramway Company had instigated a steam tram service in Birmingham on Boxing Day 1882 to Witton, but their twenty-one-year lease was due to expire on 31 December 1903. Discussions with Aston UDC led to this local council briefly becoming a somewhat reluctant steam tram operator. The UDC's operation was taken over on 1 January 1904 by CBT. All the former B&A steam tram routes were gradually converted to electric operation in stages by CBT; this was completed on 14 November 1904 when the Aston Cross–Gravelly Hill route was converted. The Lozells–Aston Station, Lichfield Road and Gravelly Hill route closed on 26 October 1904 but was operated by CBT cut-down double-deckers until 31 December 1906.

Most of the steam tram services had leases that were also due to expire on New Year's Eve 1906; these were the routes to Perry Barr, Moseley, Balsall Heath and Kings Heath, Sparkhill and Springfield, and the Wheeler Street line to Lozells. In addition the Nechells horse tram also closed at the same time.

A more complex situation occurred with regard to the Coventry Road steam tram service, which closed on 22 February 1905. After this, CBT ran electric trams between Yardley and Station Street from 23 February 1905 until their lease within Birmingham yet again expired on 31 December 1906. CBT could do this as the route from Small Heath via Hay Mills to 'The Swan' at Yardley was mostly within Yardley UDC and so seperate agreements were in place with that authority. Subsequently the whole route was jointly worked by CBT and Corporation electric cars until 31 December 1911. Finally the cable car line was closed on Friday 30 June 1911.

The City of Birmingham Tramways Company was constantly struggling financially, but was restricted by Birmingham Corporation's desire to operate their municipal tram service. Thus the constant threat of the twenty-one-year leases coming to an end made the end of the Company somewhat untidy.

Electric Trams in the Northern Area of Birmingham

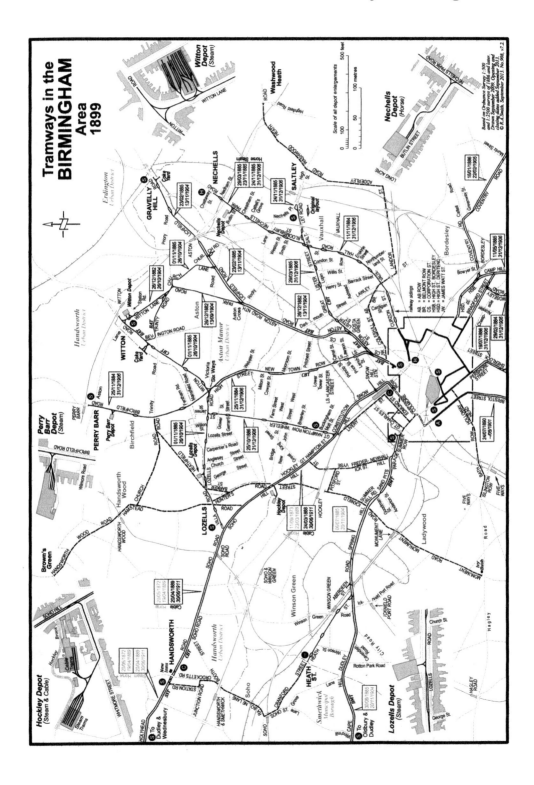

Pre-Electric Trams in the Southern Area of Birmingham

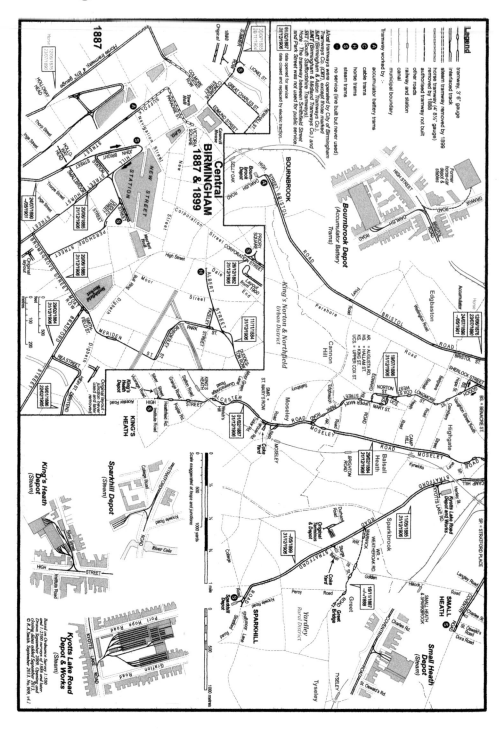

Birmingham & Aston Tramways

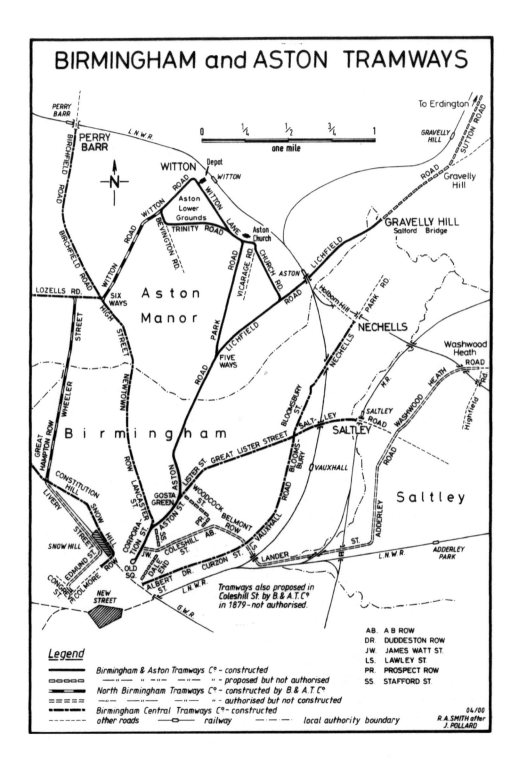

THE HEART OF STEAM TRAM
OPERATION BEFORE IT BEGAN

Old Square

The original Georgian Old Square was one of several eighteenth-century squares in the town of Birmingham and was the last one to survive in the central area. The square managed to keep its prestigious reputation for more than 100 years. Originally shops, workshops, pigsties and 'dung hills' were excluded from Old Square, but by the mid-nineteenth century, its status had declined. Although many of the original buildings survived into the 1880s as offices, the construction of Corporation Street, begun in 1876, spelled the end for this elegant square. The south side of Old Square was demolished in 1882 to make way for the construction of Corporation Street. The original Birmingham & Aston Tramways steam tram line to Witton, opened on Boxing Day 1882, terminated in a stub terminus just to the west of Upper Priory. This was replaced by a large loop around the edge of the square entering and leaving by way of Corporation Street. By the middle of the last decade of the nineteenth century, only a few of the Georgian buildings, which had previously been the epitome of the wealth and style of the well-to-do Birmingham businessman, survived in Old Square, and these were about to disappear after a long period of decline. The eighteenth-century houses including Berlin House would be replaced on the western side of the square by Newbury's huge red terracotta-faced department store, built in 1896 to the designs of Essex, Nicol and Goodman. (T. Lewis)

OLD SQUARE

The square was designed by William Westley and dates from 1713, when it was recorded as having sixteen uniform two-storied houses with five-bayed fronts having angle pilasters, pedimented doorways, and dormer windows. It was created as the centre of John Pemberton's Priory Estate development, which began in 1697. Throughout the eighteenth century, Old Square had a reputation as one of the most sought-after addresses in the town. Old Square was situated on a line from Temple Row, leading from the newly built St Philip's Church to Lichfield Street, which was the main route out of the town to the north-east. Over time it became neglected and the centre of the square itself was closed off with iron railings with several pedestrian paths. The eastern side of Old Square's Georgian buildings was already under threat of demolition by around 1895. The building with the Ionic pillars in its porticoed entrance was still the headquarters of the Birmingham Central Tramways Ltd. This company was one of the first operators of public-service vehicles in Birmingham. By 1890 BCT was responsible for steam tram services to Kings Heath, Sparkhill, Small Heath, Saltley and Perry Barr, a horse tram service to Nechells, the cable tram route to Hockley and the New Inns on the Handsworth boundary and the accumulator tram route along Bristol Road to Bournbrook. Standing next to the magnificent gaslight in the centre of Old Square are a number of barrow boys with their wicker barrows, who appear to be gossiping rather than selling any of their wares. (T. Lewis)

VICTORIA SQUARE

The impressive Council House, built in Victoria Square between 1874 and 1879 to the designs of H. R. Yeoville Thomason, dominates the skyline, towering above the Temperance Hotel owned by the Corbett family in Hill Street. This Georgian building was replaced by the General Post Office in 1891, built in the French Renaissance style. In 1886, in Victoria Square, standing beneath the statue of Sir Thomas Attwood is a Birmingham Tramways and Omnibus Co. Ltd horse tram working on Birmingham's only standard gauge track from Bournbrook on Bristol Road across the town to Hockley. The section to Hockley Brook opened on 11 September 1873 and was linked to the Bristol Road route, itself opened on 12 June 1876, during May 1879. It was the only tram route to cross the town and was abandoned in February 1887 prior to the construction of the BCT cable car route to Hockley. This horse tram route was the only one which crossed the centre of Birmingham. Its abandonment made a large gap in the town centre as trams never again penetrated so closely to the heart of Birmingham. (T. Lewis)

EARLY HORSE TRAMS

The first horse tram service in Birmingham was initiated by the Birmingham & District Tramways Company Ltd. On 11 September 1873, D & S opened the line to Handsworth on standard gauge 4-foot 8½-inch track. This was after many legal difficulties with Handsworth Council, contractors, track laying and even subsidence, as well as a delay of three days due to problems with a loop in Soho Hill. The double-deck horse trams were built by both Metropolitan RCW of Saltley and the Starbuck Car and Wagon Company of Birkenhead, and could seat thirty-six passengers split between the inside and outside passenger areas. On 1 January 1886 the BT&O Co. was taken over by Birmingham Central Tramways. The horse trams were abandoned in February 1887 and the cable cars replaced the horse trams on 24 March 1888.

Fleet No.	Manufacturer	Type	Seating	Year
1–12	Metropolitan RCW, Saltley.	4 wheel open-top double deck	20 /20	1872
13–22	Starbuck Car & Wagon Co. Ltd, Birkenhead.	4 wheel open-top double deck	18 /18	1873

At the time of the takeover by BT&O Co. Ltd, there were twenty-two trams, four omnibuses and around 100 horses.

HORSE TRAM 17

Built for the Birmingham & District Tramways Company in 1873, horse tram 17 was built by the pioneering horse tram and carriage builder Starbucks. They were based in Birkenhead where the first street tramway was opened by George Francis Train on 30 August 1860, running from Woodside Ferry on the River Mersey to Birkenhead Park. Tram 17 had a total seating capacity for thirty-six passengers and ran on standard gauge 4-foot 8½-inch-wide track. The tram is displaying a slip board for the shortworking to Villa Cross but the route did go to Holyhead Road, Handsworth. (Commercial postcard)

CABLE TRAMS

The Birmingham Central Tramways Company Ltd opened its cable tramway from Colmore Row to Hockley Brook on 24 March 1888 using the Patent Cable Tramways Corporation method of propulsion. The trams were hauled by one continuous cable on the 1½-mile route. On 20 April 1889 the second section of route to the New Inns at Crocketts Road, Handsworth, was opened. This section was operated by a second cable of around the same length as the original inward part of the route. The route was a great success and trams were still being purchased as late as 1902. The service operated for nearly twenty-three years and only came to an end when the lease to operate the line expired on 30 June 1911.

CABLE CARS

75–94	Falcon	Double-deck Open-top bogie	24/20	BCT 1888	1888–1911
95–100	Metropolitan	Double-deck 5 side windows Open-top bogie	24/20	BCT 1889	1889–1911
113–118	Falcon	Double-deck 5 side windows Open-top bogie	24/20	BCT 1896	1895–1911
119–124	Metropolitan	Double-deck 5 side windows Open-top bogie	24/20		1898–1911
141–150	CBT	Single-deck Toastrack bogie	40		1901–1904, six rebuilt to electric and to D&S 1905
172–177	CBT	Double-deck 4 side windows Open-top bogie	24/20		1902–1911

Colmore Row, Birmingham.

CABLE CAR 121

Birmingham Central operated fifty-three cable cars belonging to six classes. This is car 121, which was one of the 119-124 Class built by the Metropolitan Company in 1889 for the Handsworth extension. Metropolitan had pioneered the steel under framed-bogie cars for steam tram trailers, and the cable cars built at this time were very similar. Cable car 121 is standing in Colmore Row alongside St Philip's Churchyard in the early years of the twentieth-century, waiting to move off to Hockley Brook. Just visible at the end of Colmore Row are the Corinthian pillars of J. A. Hansom's town hall, the construction of which was begun in 1832 and the first concert held there in 1834. (Commercial postcard)

COLMORE ROW

Colmore Row has had various names in its history, but originally most of its length was called Ann Street after Ann Colmore, whose family owned the land on the ridge to the north of the growing town and gave the land for St Philip's Church, which was later to become Birmingham Cathedral. The eastern end was called Monmouth Street and the original Birmingham station opened by the Great Western Railway in 1852 had this name, only becoming Snow Hill Station some years later. The area grew in the early years of the eighteenth century to become the fashionable location for the stylish residences of leading merchants and the newly wealthy manufacturers. In spite of the rapid expansion of the town from the late eighteenth century, and the growth of industrial development, the Colmore Estate lands remained the area in which the wealthy people of Birmingham retained their gracious town houses. After 1866, when the leases of the buildings in Ann Street came up for renewal, a start was made on widening the road and it was renamed Colmore Row. The Georgian terraces were being swept away in around 1875 and the road was widened, with the impressive edifices built on the new alignment of Colmore Row. The splendid row of buildings opposite St Philip's Cathedral make up the Grand Hotel on the corner of Church Street, which was one of the first of the new generation to be completed, in 1875 to the design of Thomson Plevins. It was into this new environment that the BCT cable trams entered on 24 March 1888. A distant CBT cable tram stands just beyond the junction of Livery Street at the terminus in Colmore Row. Beyond the iron railings around St Philip's Churchyard, on the right, is the Blue Coat School's original 1794 building, which was demolished in 1935 when the school moved out of the city centre to Harborne. (Commercial postcard)

CABLE CAR 150

Waiting in Colmore Row near to the Blue Coat School is one of the more bizarre purchases by any tram operator in the United Kingdom. Notwithstanding that it was a cable car, the City of Birmingham Tramways Company purchased ten single-deck toast-rack trams built in 1899/1900 by the CBT Company, in its Kyott's Lake Road Works, as bogie cable cars. These were numbered 141–150 and were constructed for summer use, though in hindsight it does seem a strange decision to build them at all. The 33-foot-long cars in their original condition had the normal cable-car type of widely spaced bogies, above which were the gripper operating handle and brake wheel on both of the very short platforms. Behind the driver, in front of a full-width bulkhead, was a single bench seat. Six of the ten toast-rack cable trams were taken out of service in 1904, and reconstructed as electric trams with a pair of Brush 1002B 32-hp motors and mounted on Lycett & Conaty Brush Radial trucks. They were briefly used on the Aston Cross to Gravelly Hill electric service after the closure of the CBT steam tram service as these former cable cars were able to work underneath Aston Station bridge prior to its rebuilding. They were subsequently sent to the Kinver Light Railway whereupon they were renumbered in the Dudley & Stourbridge fleet number series 63–68.

CABLE CAR 84

The impressive frontage of Snow Hill Station was completed as part of the 120-room Great Western Hotel in 1863. The railway station behind it dated from 1871 and had become a somewhat shabby place until it was rebuilt by the Great Western Railway, reopening during January 1912 after a reconstruction and enlargement that took nearly six years to complete. The old station buildings on the platforms located alongside Livery Street are still visible near to the parked hansom cabs. In around 1899 a CBT cable tram, car 84, moves along Colmore Row and is about to make the left-hand turn into Snow Hill. This open-top bogie car was built by Falcon in 1888 as one of the first batch of twenty trailers in the original cable-car fleet numbered 75–94. On the right, travelling along Colmore Row towards the cathedral, is a horse bus. There are three horses pulling the bus rather than the usual two because of the steepness of Snow Hill. This third horse was known as a trace horse.

CABLE CAR AT THE GREAT WESTERN ARCADE

Waiting at its terminus in Colmore Row is one of the City of Birmingham Tramways Falcon-bodied double-decker bogie cable cars, which had operated to Hockley and beyond to the New Inns at Crocketts Lane, Handsworth, since the service began on 24 March 1888. It appears that all the passengers on the open-top deck are either women or girls, all wearing wide-brimmed hats to protect them from the sun. The tram is outside the entrance to the Great Western Arcade, opposite Snow Hill station's entrance, as a lone cyclist pedals up the hill in front of the tram into Colmore Row from the top of Snow Hill in around 1905. The Great Western Arcade had been opened over the railway tunnel leading into the newly rebuilt Snow Hill station in 1876. It had been designed by W. H. Ward, and its impressive Renaissance-style frontage hid an airy, refined interior, with balconies, elegant chandeliers, tiling and wood panelling. It was reached through the large arch to the left of H. Beresford's music publishers and sheet music suppliers. Beyond the other side of the entrance is Steele's hairdressing salon, where a haircut would cost 4d and a shave 2d. Next door, towards Bull Street, is the earlier Italianate-style Great Western Vaults public house. The walls of the pub are plastered with advertisements for Symington's Coffee Essence, Nestlé's Swiss Milk, Colman's Starch and Bliss's Hats, among others. The last-named was based in premises at the top of Snow Hill, and the advertisement suggests that they had the patronage of no less a person than King Edward VII.

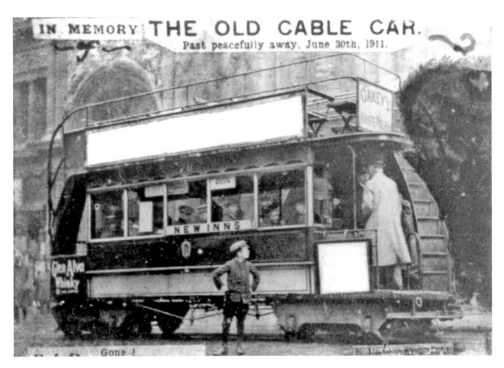

IN MEMORY THE OLD CABLE CAR.
Past peacefully away, June 30th, 1911.

Gone !

Cable Car 76

The second of the original Falcon open-top bogie cars of 1888, car 76, waits in front of the Great Western Arcade in Colmore Row in 1911. Within the Great Western Arcade were a variety of high-quality clothiers, as well as furriers, shoe shops, jewellers and drapers. The cable cars were rather successful and operated for nearly twenty-three years, but had to close when the lease to operate the line expired on 30 June 1911. Many such valedictory postcards were produced at this time to commemorate the enforced closure of the cable cars with this card having '*In Memory*', '*RIP*', '*Past peacefully away*' and '*Poor Old Cable Car. Thy work is done, you were a good servant when you could run, still in our memory you'll ever be dear*'. Well, it's hardly Shakespeare but perhaps does show that the Handsworth cable trams were well liked. Strangely when the last Birmingham City Transport electric trams were abandoned on 4 July 1953 they were adorned with comments written on their panels in chalk which were very similar to those of 1911. Another valedictory postcard carried the following poem:

Farewell, kind friends, I'm going/ To the scrap heap, so they say:/ The worthy City Fathers/ Think too long I've held the sway./ They deem me old and ugly,/ In fact, not up to date:/ If ever love they had for me/ Their love's turned into hate./ This city's known as "Foreward"/ A motto that means well:/ 'Tis that what makes them anxious/ The cable car to sell./ Some say that I'm not handsome,/ But most of them agree/ When electric cars they take my place/ Improvement there will be./ And now before I leave you/ Kind friends take my advice:/ And you, both guards and drivers/ Who all have acted nice –/ Give out a hearty welcome/ When the new friend does appear:/ For though his name's Electric Car/ To you welfare he's sincere

(C. Carter)

CAR 116

Travelling down Snow Hill in around 1905 is CBT cable car 116. This open-top bogie car was built by Metropolitan RCW in 1898, and seated twenty-four passengers outside and twenty longitudinally in the lower saloon. The central slot between the running rails is for the cable, which was gripped by the tram in order for it to move. The second Great Western Railway Station at Snow Hill was still in use, as the removal of the large single-span iron roof only began in 1907, and one of the advertisements is a sign for the GWR and the Great Central Railway jointly operating the alternative route between Princes Risborough and High Wycombe, which only began operating in 1906.

SNOW HILL (*Opposite above*)

The CBT cable trams to Handsworth were forced to close on 30 June 1911 when their operating lease ended. The following day Birmingham Corporation Tramways took over the operating of the route and in early July 1911 there were still some granite setts being laid between the newly laid electric tram tracks below the electric overhead tram wiring. After the rebuilding of Snow Hill Station was completed, the steep descent of Snow Hill was all the more noticeable from the top of Snow Hill junction because of the increasingly high wall of brickwork in Snow Hill necessary to ensure the railway station's level formation across the distant Great Charles Street and the valley of the tiny Fleet Brook. The women outside the side entrance to the station are waiting at a newly installed Corporation ALL TRAMS STOP HERE red plate stop. The tram track in the foreground connected the termini in Colmore Row to the left and Steelhouse Lane to the right, and was in use from 1911 until 1939.

CABLE TRAM TRACK LAYING IN SNOW HILL

Looking from Slaney Street, nearly opposite Great Charles Street, up Snow Hill towards Colmore Row, the cable conduit and tram tracks are being laid in early 1888. Slaney Street was named after an eighteenth-century Birmingham family and the area led back into Steelhouse Lane. The original 1871 Snow Hill station buildings are just visible beyond the wall of advertisements on the billboards, while on the left are the mainly early Victorian buildings, which were all converted to retail premises. The sheer labour intensity of undertaking this civil engineering project is staggering, not least because the main tools used were picks and shovels.

Constitution Hill

Not a cable tramcar in sight, but there is cable conduit between the rails. This is Constitution Hill looking towards the Hockley end of Livery Street in around 1895, and the state of the early nineteenth-century buildings appears to put them in terminal decline; residential property had already been converted into manufacturing premises, as had occurred in the nearby Jewellery Quarter. Yet the last building on the left before the advertising hoardings on the corner of Northwood Street is a public house called the White Horse Cellars. The pub dated from between 1885 and 1890 and occupies the corner site into Northwood Street. This three-storey red-brick building is a Grade II listed building. Beyond this point was the turn into Great Hampton Row. Opened on 25 October 1886, this was covered by BCT with their steam tram service to Lozells. Once the cable-car service to the New Inns had started, the steam trams were incompatible with the track, which resulted in the town end terminus being cut back to the junction of Great Hampton Row and Constitution Hill and the connecting curve from the out-of-town track in Constitution Hill into Great Hampton Row being removed. (Birmingham CRL)

Hockley Brook (*Opposite below*)

A CBT cable tram negotiates the gap between the end of the Birmingham–Hockley Brook cable and the Hockley Brook–New Inns, Handsworth cable. The tram's driver had to be skilled in order to coast across the short gap between the two cables. The tram is on its way out of Birmingham towards Handsworth. To the left is the junction with Icknield Street, with the Turks Head public house on its corner. Dominating Hockley Brook at the junction of Hunters Road is Hockley House with its striped canvas sunblinds extended. It was occupied by D. A. Tipper, who was a draper. On the right, behind the cart, is the Benyon Arms public house; beyond the cable tramcar on Soho Hill is the spire of Soho Hill Congregational chapel, which was built in 1892. (Commercial postcard)

LAYING THE CABLE

It is difficult to definitely identify this location, but it is probably Hockley Brook. It must date from the early months of 1888. The cable is on a large calender, which in turn is mounted on a large pair of wheels. Work is progressing in the roadway with a trench having already been dug and lined with an iron channel prior to the insertion of the cable. Unlike the photos in Snow Hill, the contractor's labourers seem to be working steadily rather than with any urgency!

CAR 81

All the CBT cable trams were open-top, forty-eight-seater bogie cars. Car 81 is standing outside the Cable Tramway Inn in July 1890. Car 81 was built in 1888 as one of the first twenty cable cars, numbered 75–94 by the Falcon Engine & Car Works of Loughborough, who became the better-remembered Brush Electrical Engineering Company during the following year. The curved track in the foreground led to the tram depot in nearby Whitmore Street where there was a large winding house with a steam-winding engine for each of the two cables that met in Hockley Brook. The trams gripped the moving continuous loops of steel cable, which ran on pulleys in a slot between the running rails. This was controlled by means of a lever on the platform, the cable running at a speed of 9 mph. Starting and stopping tended to be very jerky, and the cables tended to break. Nevertheless, the system continued to operate successfully for twenty-three years.

Single-Deck, Open Cross-Bench Cable Car

Parked in Hockley depot yard is one of the Hockley cable tramway's toast-rack trams built between 1899 and 1900, which received fleet Nos 141–150. In 1904, six of these were withdrawn and reconstructed at the same works as open electric cars, being then renumbered in that company's electric car series, as 257–262. It is assumed that it was intended to use these cars on the CBT system, at that time, although on what services such a type of car would have been suitable in an industrial city is something of a mystery. It is known, however, that two at least of them were used on electric services through Aston station bridge, prior to the completion of its reconstruction in April 1906. Several of the rebuilt cars began to operate on the Kinver line during 1905, and by 1906/7 it appears that all six were in use there. It has been suggested that, during their life as electric trams, until the closure of the CBT in 1911, these cars may have been actually operated by the latter company purely for the excursion traffic to Kinver, working from a depot in the Birmingham area. As toast racks, the full-width seating of the open passenger section was of the back-to-back type, there being four double benches, plus a single one against each bulkhead. The roof was of the domed type and carried a small, fixed destination board on top of each end canopy. A full-length side step was provided on each side. As reconstructed for electric traction, the car bodies were basically untouched but for modifications to make them suitable for electric use, although a number of these electrified toastracks were further rebuilt as totally enclosed single-deck saloons.

Steam Locomotive 89 (*Opposite below*)

The BCT cable trams were shedded at Hockley depot, but did have the problem in getting from the depot in Whitmore Street, Hockley, to the main line in Hockley Brook where they could pick up either the cable to Colmore Row or the outer cable to the New Inns in Handsworth. The main difficulty was that the trams could not get between the depot and the route under their own power. This was enabled by the use of a steam locomotive, which was used as a depot shunter to manoeuvre the cable cars around the depot and to Hockley Brook. Tram 89 was an Improved Kitson locomotive and dated from 1898; it would survive until the closure of the CBT steam tram operation on New Year's Eve 1906. (Whitcombe Collection)

Trams 546 and 615

Hockley tram depot was built in 1888 for the Birmingham Central Tramways Co. to house their fleet of cable cars. The depot housed all fifty-three cable trams, and ran them from this depot until the original twenty-one-year lease expired. On the expiry of the lease, Birmingham Corporation Tramways took over the operation of the Handsworth line on 1 July 1911, having converted the line to overhead electric tram operation. While Hockley depot was slowly converted to electric tram operation, the tram routes were operated from Miller Street depot until Hockley was reopened on 12 June 1912. It was doubled in size, with eight roads and a capacity for eighty-eight trams. The original offices, stationery and ticket office, and generator plant were in the siding on the right where UEC-bogie tramcar 546 stands. The tram parked in Row 1 of the garage on 1 March 1939 is Brush-built car 615 of 1920. The trams in the foreground led across the depot forecourt to the exit into Whitmore Street. A month later the trams would be replaced by buses on the through routes via Handsworth to West Bromwich, Wednesbury and Dudley. (R. T. Coxon)

Buses 2140 and 3172 (*Opposite above*)

The long-since-abandoned tram tracks and cobbles are still seen her in situ in around 1966, and would remain undisturbed until Hockley bus garage was closed by the National Express Group in May 2005. Standing just inside the old tram roads 4 and 5 is 2140, (JOJ 140), a 1949 Leyland 'Titan' PD2/1 with a Leyland H30/26R body. There were fifty of these buses, which spent their entire lives at Hockley garage, with 2140 being one of the longest-lived of these stalwarts, not being withdrawn until December 1968. Alongside it is 3172, (MOF 172), a Crossley-bodied 'new look front' Daimler CVG6 dating from March 1954.

SOHO HILL

In around 1904, a CBT cable car climbs the steep Soho Hill as it approaches the forked junction with Hamstead Road. Occupying that angled corner is the Roebuck Public House. Just visible to the left of the pub is an inbound cable car that is about to descend the hill. Having left Hockley Brook on the second continuous cable, the ascending cable tram is on its way to the New Inns at Handsworth. The west side of the main road is occupied by early nineteenth-century houses, which were swept away in the mid-1960s when Hockley flyover was built. Dominating the east side of Soho Hill is the rather ungainly tower on top of Soho Hill Congregational chapel, built in 1892. On the right, with the decorative brickwork, is the gilt jewellery and stud manufacturer Sydney Griffith. (Commercial postcard)

CAR 176 (*Opposite above*)

As the horse and cart comes out of Villa Road, cable car 176 stands at the junction at the top of Soho Hill. This was built for the City of Birmingham Tramways in 1902 as one of their final six cable cars for the Handsworth service. Numbered 172–177, these double-deck open-top forty-four-seat bogie trams were constructed by CBT at Kyotts Lake Road works with a capacity of twenty-four outside and twenty in the lower saloon. The cable car is passing the Old Gate Glass and China Repository building, which dated from the 1880s.

CARS 81 AND 124 (*Opposite below*)

Metropolitan C&W car 124 of 1898 travels on an outward journey along Soho Road near to the L&NWR station of the same name, and passes the earlier Falcon-built tram dating from 1888. In the distance is the large shop at the junction with Villa Road. The driver of 124 looks imperiously down the road in front of him wondering if he can squeeze past the horse and cart, while on the rear platform of the inbound car, the conductor appears to be about to begin to collect fares in the lower saloon. To the right of the bustling pedestrians, the shops that can be identified include a Thomas Cook 'Tourist Office' and a cycle repair shop.

CAR 175 (*Top*)

CBT-built four-bay-construction cable tramcar 175, built in 1902, is travelling towards Hockley Brook and is at the junction of Soho Hill and Hamstead Road. Similar cable trams in Edinburgh of this vintage were converted to electric traction, but these CBT cars were not so fortunate. It would appear that at this time CBT was content to continue operating the cable-car route from Colmore Row to the New Inns when they bought this final batch of trams, but on 8 October 1909 Handsworth UDC bought the line from Hockley Brook to the New Inns. As the city had resolved to electrify their inner section when the lease expired on 30 June 1911, this spelled the end for the cable car system, leaving car 176 to be scrapped after only nine years of life. (Commercial postcard)

Cars 94 and 95

Cable car 95 is picking up passengers outside Handsworth Council House in Soho Road in around 1901. This cable car was the first of the second batch of cable trams to enter service for the opening of the second cable from Hockley Brook to the New Inns, Handsworth boundary on 20 May 1889. The cable car was constructed by the Metropolitan Carriage & Wagon Works in Saltley, and was one of just five extra cable trams required for the increase in traffic on the new section. Coming out of Hockley is car 94, which was the last of the original twenty cable cars built in 1888 by Falcon for the original inner half of the route from Colmore Row. Both trams, albeit built by different manufacturers, were of the same basic design, although there are detailed difference in the design of the dash panels, staircase and sundry handrails. Precisely what the driver of one of the trams is doing jumping from one platform to another is long forgotten, but he does appear to be emptying the contents of a box from car 95 onto the platform of car 94.

Car 89 (*Opposite above*)

Another of the original twenty trams is car 89. Built by the Falcon Co. of Loughborough in 1888 as an open-top bogie double-decker, it is travelling past Council House through the already developing shopping centre in Soho Road towards Hockley around the end of the Victorian period. The cables on both halves of the route ran at 9 mph, which meant that for most of their lives the cable trams were faster than the rest of the traffic, which, as is patently obvious, was horse-drawn. The impressive building was designed by A. E. Henman and built in red brick and terracotta with stone dressings and a slate roof. The two-storey building has a steeply pitched roof and an impressive clock tower, and was opened by 1879 as the Urban Districts Council's offices. Ten years later the second half of the CBT cable tram route was opened from Hockley to the New Inns. (C. Carter)

CAR 172

Metropolitan RCW-built tram rumbles along Soho Road with its driver controlling the speed by dexterous use of his brake handle, which gripped or released the cable as required. The tram is passing Handsworth Council House, whose foundation stone was laid on 30 October 1877 on the site of an old inn called the Waggon & Horses. This building represented Handsworth's civic pride and fierce independence from nearby Birmingham, and cost £14,000, which included the interior fixtures and furnishings. It was built on the corner of Stafford Road on the opposite corner to the Frighted Horse public house. This originally sold Cheshire's Windmill Ales but was taken over in 1912 by Mitchells & Butlers just around the time when everything else changed in Handsworth for ever. Beyond the distant carts and the tall trees are the two-storeyed Rhodes almshouses, which date from 1872, built in a Jacobean style in brick with stone dressings. (Commercial postcard)

Car 86

On a hot summer's day, with Handsworth Council House looming over Soho Road, the shops all have their canvas blinds pulled out over the pavement, and car 86 approaches the junction with Grove Lane. This was one of the original batch of twenty Falcon double-deck open-top bogie cars of 1888, built for the Birmingham Central Tramways Co. The building with the Dutch gable was for many years used as a gas appliance showroom while the small garden wall to the right of the parked horse and carts survived into the 1930s.

CAR 177

Numerically the last of the cable cars supplied to CBT in 1902 was car 177, which is climbing Holyhead Road towards the terminus at the New Inns public house at the junction with Crocketts Road. It is travelling away from the distant Booth Street junction on Holyhead Road in around 1905 and is passing the Ashbury Memorial Chapel located on the corner of Milestone Lane, whose spire towers over the surrounding houses. The chapel was named after Francis Ashbury, who was born in Newton Road in the late eighteenth century and later became a founder of the Methodist Episcopal Church of America. This cable car was one of the five built at Kyotts Lake Road works in 1902. They were the last non-electric trams to be built by CBT and were constructed after the CBT electric cars 166–171, built in 1901 for the conversion of the Bristol Road route from accumulator cars to overhead electric trams. From this it can be seen that CBT had a continuous fleet numbering scheme, which began at number 1 in 1884 with the first of the Falcon steam tram trailers and ended in 1905 with fourteen electric four-wheelers, built by Brush and numbered 243–256. Admittedly, the six toast racks converted to electric from cable operation were briefly numbered 257–262, but they were soon renumbered again as 63–68 in the Dudley & Stourbridge fleet for use on the Kinver Light Railway. (Commercial postcard)

CABLE CAR (*Opposite below*)

Soho Road is lined with a positive throng who are watching a convoy of fancy dressed cyclists pedal across the Grove Lane junction in Soho Road. With the buildings adorned with bunting on a summer's day, it can only be to celebrate the delayed coronation of King Edward VII, which took place, after the king had collapsed with appendicitis two months before, at Westminster Abbey on 9 August 1902. In the distance, a cable car, standing roughly opposite Handsworth Council House, waits well behind the last of the cyclists.

CAR 95

The first of the five double-deck five side windows forty-four-seater open-top bogie cars built by the Metropolitan RCW on 1889 stands opposite the New Inns in Holyhead Road. It is parked just beyond St James's Road and in front of the short row of shops that went up to Crocketts Road. The smartly uniformed driver and conductor stand on the front platform, having just arrived from Hockley. The plate-framed equal-wheel bogies on these cars were placed at the extreme ends of the platforms in order to give a better ride on the somewhat hard-riding springs. The track brake blocks have been applied in order to stop the tram from running back down the hill in Holyhead Road.

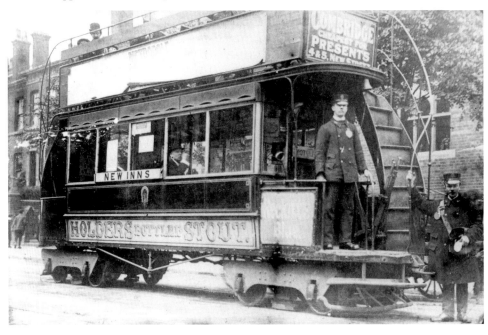

New Inns

The terminus of the CBT cable cars was the New Inns, Handsworth, on the corner of Sandwell Road and Crocketts Road. The second half of the route was opened from Hockley on 20 April 1889. Although neither of the two cable cars is identifiable, the left is one of the 1888 Falcon-built trams while the one on the right is a 1902-vintage CBT-built tram. The New Inns, a Mitchells & Butlers-owned public house, in this form, was not opened until 1901 when it replaced a much older inn, parts of which had been built in 1638. The brewery extended the property in 1904 when the Assembly Rooms were opened, which are on the right of the cable tram. Throughout the 1980s it remained derelict, but most of the building was eventually saved and converted into flats by November 1995. In the distance on the other side of Crocketts Road are two South Staffordshire open-top electric bogie trams. (Commercial postcard)

Car 96 (*Opposite below*)

Parked in Holyhead Road, just short of St James's Road and facing the terminus, is Metropolitan RCW cable car 96. The smartly uniformed platform staff pose at the front end of the cable car, with the conductor wearing a great coat beneath his leather cash satchel. On the rocker panel of the tram's body is a painted advertisement for Holders bottled stout in Nova Scotia Street, just north of Curzon Street Station. Holder's Brewery was founded in around 1872 by John Charles Holder and was based at the Midland Brewery in Nova Scotia Street. This was just inside the boundary between Birmingham and Aston, and for a time was one of the premier breweries in Birmingham. The company was acquired by Mitchell's and Butler's in 1919 and the Midland Brewery was closed in 1923. (Commercial postcard)

Cable Cars at New Inns

Parked opposite the New Inns, just short of the Crocketts Road junction at the end of the row of Victorian buildings on the left, in around 1905 are three CBT cable cars. The New Inns Public House was rebuilt for Mitchell & Butlers in 1901, though its huge Assembly Room was not finished until 1904. One of the features of the building was its large and distinctive clock, which must have been a most useful aid for the platform staff working on the cable cars. The interior was decorated with art nouveau ceramic tiles, and its opulence made it one of the gems of interior public house design in the Birmingham area, and as such a prime venue for weddings and other important functions. (Commercial Postcard)

BRISTOL ROAD HORSE TRAM

The original tram route was operated by the Birmingham Tramway & Omnibus Co. Ltd and was operated from 5 June 1876 on 4-foot 8½-inch-gauge track. The route ran from Navigation Street, via Suffolk Street, the Horse Fair, Bristol Street and along Bristol Road, through Edgbaston before arriving at its terminus in Bournbrook at Grange Road. This company was taken over by Birmingham Central on 1 January 1886 and continued operation until 11 July 1889 when it was discontinued in order that the standard gauge track could be lifted and replaced by the 3-foot 6-inch gauge for the accumulator trams. Until the battery electric trams could be introduced, the Bristol Road service was maintained by CBT horse buses.

Fleet No.	Manufacturer	Type	Seating	Year
1–22	Metropolitan RCW, Saltley.	4 wheel open-top double deck	20 /20	1876
23–27	?	?	?	1876
28–29	Starbuck Car & Wagon Co. Ltd, Birkenhead.	4 wheel open single - deck	40	19/4/1878
30	Brown Marshalls & Co. Ltd, Birmingham.	4 wheel open-top double deck	22 /20	11/1878
31–34	Hughes Locomotive Tramway Engine Works Ltd Eades reversible		?/? 45	1879

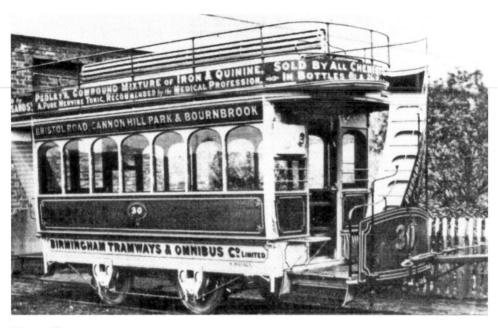

HORSE TRAM 30

Horse tram number 30 was built by Brown, Marshalls & Co. Ltd of Birmingham in around 1876 as a one-off for the Standard Guage route along Bristol Road as most of the others in the BT&O Co. were supplied by either the Metropolitan RCW Company or Starbucks. The basic route was painted on the cantrail above the Gothic-arched saloon windows, and the service terminated at the junction with Grange Road where in later years the Ariel Motorcycle Company was located. The stables for the horse trams survived well into the 1970s.

ACCUMULATOR TRAMS

Although the Birmingham Central Tramways Company had firmly established the operation of steam tramcars since 1884 on six routes, they chose the cable system for their Handsworth tram service. This was purely on the grounds that it was the only method of propulsion powerful enough to pull the tramcars over the steeply undulating terrain that the old turnpike road followed. When BCT proposed an electric tram system along Bristol Road to Bournbrook using overhead current collection, this was turned down both by Birmingham Council and by the influential and wealthy Gough-Calthorpe family whose estate the route would pass. The Elwell-Parker Company of Wolverhampton had experimented with a self-contained battery-powered locomotive using a new alloy invented by a Belgian engineer named Edmund Julien. This locomotive was delivered to BCT in 1888 and cost £700. The locomotive was paired with BCT bogie cable car 90, which had its cable equipment removed and was used to demonstrate that the battery locomotive could haul a fully laden passenger trailer. The trials were undertaken from the depot in Kyotts Lake Road in Sparkbrook on Monday 1 October 1888, but a succession of chain drive failures when climbing the steep 1 in 17 hill in Bradford Street led to it being used on test runs on other steam track routes. It was purchased by BCT sometime during 1889, but was relegated to shunting duties at Dawlish Road depot after the recently opened accumulator car service began on 24 July 1890. It was also used as the Hockley depot shunter, temporarily replacing a steam tram locomotive for a few years before quietly fading away, probably because of battery failure in around 1892. But it had proved the point that, despite inadequate recharging facilities at Kyotts Lake Road depot, battery power could be made to work.

After the trials with 'The Julien' locomotive, initially eight accumulator trams were purchased and car 101, which had been delivered as early as 23 October 1889, was trialled on the route to Sparkbrook. Guests were carried on the tram on 30 October and the order was increased by four to make up the new fleet to twelve trams to be numbered 101–112. The service began on 24 June 1890 but problems were to appear quickly. In their first year, the cost per car mile was only 9.90*d*, which was less than steam tram operation but considerably more than the Handsworth cable trams, which cost only 6.33*d* per car mile.

A Mr Henry Lea, who was a consulting engineer, was employed to oversee any possible problems with these new, revolutionary trams. The first problem that Mr Lea encountered was faulty linkages to the brake handles; this was soon overcome by the fitting of handbrake wheels on the platforms. There were failures with the brass bushes in the motors wearing away and the corroding of the battery boxes on the trams due to acid corrosion. Passengers complained about acid fumes and occasional damage to clothing, and gradually, with battery plates buckling, short circuits caused more maintenance problems, with the cost per car mile reaching 15.61d per mile by 1892. The cars were re-equipped with new Epstein Electric Accumulator Company solid lead castings from August 1892, which initially made a marked improvement regarding service frequency and reliability, and battery longevity. Yet by 1894 the Epstein batteries were again receiving the same complaints by passengers, and the cost per car mile had gone up to 17.08d.

Meanwhile the Electrical Power Storage Company, using its own and the Julien patents, produced an improved battery, and during 1894 BCT placed an order for ten car sets. It was during 1894 that BCT applied to Birmingham Corporation to reconstruct the Bristol Road tramway to overhead current collection. A visit was made to Walsall to inspect the South Staffordshire Tramway Company's pioneering overhead route, which had opened on 1 January 1893, but after considering all the facts, the Corporation turned down the request on the grounds of the unsightly overhead, a reason much quoted in later years when the Calthorpe Estate fought long and hard against the Corporation's proposal for trams along Hagley Road. Yet by mid-1896 the line was quoted as having comfortable trams and well-maintained permanent way, and it was said that the trams moved 'smoothly and reliably'. The only criticism was that it did not pay! The costs were now up to 20.6d per car mile and in the final year of BCT the accumulator trams made a net loss of £1,735. The new company, the City of Birmingham Tramways Co. Ltd, was formed on 29 September 1896 out of the financially ruined BCT operation. CBT made several attempts to again persuade the Corporation to allow them to convert the line to overhead current collection, and in early 1900 it was successful, leading to the much vaunted conversion on 14 May 1901.

The Tramway Company and the ECC should be accorded considerable credit for having made an early technical success of battery traction, despite formidable problems due to the lack of knowledge of accumulators and of drive systems at the time. To have operated the line for eleven years, far longer than any other accumulator tramway in this country, was indeed an amazing achievement.

101–112	Falcon	Double-deck Open-top bogie. 6 side windows ECC electrics	27/24		1890–1901
113 demonstrator	Brown Marshall	Double-deck Open-top four-wheel. 4 side windows. ECC electrics	20/14		1892–1894
114 demonstrator	Brown Marshall	Double-deck Open-top four wheel. 4 side windows GEP electrics	20/14		1892–1894

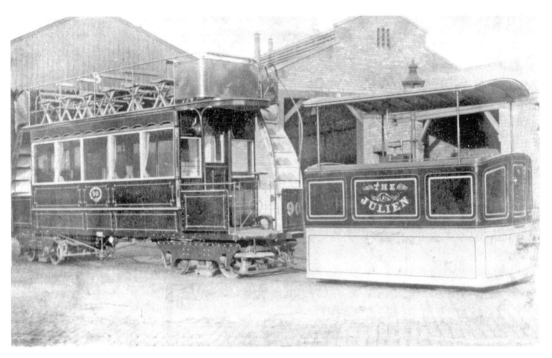

THE JULIEN

The locomotive was named 'The Julien' after the Belgian engineer who invented it and weighed some 8 tons, though a contemporary steam tram was heavier at around 14 tons.

'The Julien' locomotive and cable car 90 stand on the forecourt of Hockley depot during the period of the trials on Stratford Road, which lasted some ten months and resulted in BCT confirming their order for twelve self-contained accumulator trams for the new Bristol Road service.

ACCUMULATOR CAR 104

The terminus of the accumulator tramcar route to Bournbrook was in Suffolk Street at the junction with Navigation Street. The preceding horse tram service continued up the hill to Paradise Street and then into Victoria Square, joining up with the Hockley horse tram route. The operation of battery accumulator trams along Bristol Road to Dawlish Road, Bournbrook, began on 24 July 1890 and was deemed successful, despite the necessity to recharge the banks of twelve batteries twice a day and CBT's original wish to operate overhead electric trams. The batteries were housed behind six panels on each side of the tram, and occupied the area underneath the lower saloon behind the rocker panels. The route was 3 miles long and took sixteen minutes from Suffolk Street to Dawlish Road, Bournbrook. Car 104 was constructed by the Falcon Company of Loughborough; these bogie cars were 26 feet 6 inches long and had a seating capacity of twenty-four inside and twenty-six outside. (A. Jenson)

CAR 103 (*Opposite above*)

Travelling towards the city terminus in Suffolk Street is CBT car 103. It is standing in the Horse Fair almost at the junction with Holloway Head. The wide Horse Fair was used, as its name implies, for a once-a-week animal livestock market, which continued until after the abandonment of the accumulator tram service. The building on the right was occupied by a paint manufacturer and later used by a leather goods manufacturer. Just behind the tram was the Duke of York Public House. The tall building beyond the pub is St Catherine of Sienna Roman Catholic Church, originally built in 1875. The Malt Shovel Public House stood in the apex of the junction of Suffolk Street to the left and John Bright Street to the right. The pub had been opened in 1883 and was renamed The Argyle in 1903.

HORSE FAIR AND SUFFOLK STREET

Looking towards the city centre from the Horse Fair in the mid-1890s, a CBT accumulator car unloads in front of the Malt Shovel public house. From this angle the gradient of Suffolk Street, which carried the accumulator trams to their terminus, can be appreciated. Criticism of these battery trams in their later years of service concerned the supposed spillage of acid from the batteries, particularly on to ladies' long dresses. However, these criticisms were made largely in order to discredit the accumulator cars and encourage the CBT Co. to convert the Bournbrook service to overhead electric cars, which they had originally intended in 1891. One of the accumulator trams, possibly car 106, drops off passengers while the woman and her little daughter wearing a smock dress wait to board for the short journey to the Suffolk Street terminus. On the right is smoke coming from one of the CBT steam trams on its way to Kings Heath before the route from Hill Street was reversed.

Birmingham Corporation Trams 543 and 560

The last tram stop in Horse Fair was just short of the junction of Smallbrook Street (to the right) and Holloway Head (beyond the tall building to the left) and was located in the middle of this important thoroughfare. Although the photograph was taken in 1949, the street hadn't significantly changed since the Edwardian period. Car 543 a totally enclosed bogie car is inbound on the 71 route from Rubery and will take the tracks into Suffolk Street after passing outward-bound car 560, coming out of John Bright Street on the 35 route shortworking to Selly Oak.

Car 108 (*Opposite above*)

There had been a horse fair and associated market held in Birmingham at the town end of Bristol Street since 1777, in what originally had been called Brick Kiln Lane. The site became the main place for horse trading during the latter part of the Napoleonic Wars, so not long after 1812 the street between Holloway Head and Essex Street was renamed Horse Fair. Horse Fair survived well into the early years of the twentieth century as a horse market, and only really fell out of use when horses began to be replaced by motorised vehicles in the middle of the Edwardian period. In Horse Fair in around 1895 young children, some quite smartly dressed and others in fairly ragged clothing and without shoes, stroke the horses and ponies, which are all tagged with their sale price and ready to meet their buyers. Beyond the canvas awning on the left is the Smallbrook Street junction at the bottom of Holloway Head, with the Bull's Head public house on the corner. Travelling through Horse Fair is car 108, one of CBT's twelve battery-operated open-topped bogie tramcars built by the Falcon Company of Loughborough for the opening of the new service on 24 July 1890 between Suffolk Street and Dawlish Road, Bournbrook. The tram is carrying an advertisement for Sala's Skin Lotion, which at 1s was an expensive luxury. The Bristol Road route was the most successful and longest-lasting operation of battery-powered trams in this country, and was replaced by CBT's new fleet of small overhead electric trams on Tuesday 14 May 1901.

CBT 166

There are no known photographs of the accumulator trams between Bristol Street and Bournbrook, but there are early views of the first CBT electric trams travelling along Bristol Road in the area of Sir Harry's Road within the first few years of operation. The only real gradient on the route is in the distance behind the tram. This was a 1 in 30 climb from Belgrave Road to Balsall Heath, which was well within the compass of the accumulator trams. Car 166 was built in 1901 at the CBT works in Kyotts Lake Road. They were only forty-eight-seaters and were mounted on Peckham 6-foot-long cantilever trucks. This tramcar was transferred to Birmingham Corporation Tramways on 1 July 1911 when the lease to the CBT Bristol Road and Pershore Road routes expired. Car 166 is travelling towards Selly Oak at Sir Harry's Road in around 1904. (C. Carter)

CAR 106

The Birmingham Central Tramways Company began operating battery accumulator tramcars from the Suffolk Street junction with Navigation Street to Dawlish Road, Bournbrook, on 24 July 1890. Cars 101–112 were eight-wheel open-top bogie trams built by the Falcon Engine & Car Works of Loughborough, and carried twenty-seven passengers outside on tip-over garden seats, and twenty-four people on the longitudinal seats in the lower saloon. At first glance they looked similar to the contemporary cable cars running on the route to Hockley and Handsworth, although the six panels in the tram's rocker sheet were where the rechargeable traction batteries were housed. Car 106 is parked at the terminus in Bristol Road, just short of the turn into the depot located in Dawlish Road, and is about to leave for Birmingham. On the front platform is the driver and wheels on the platform operate the brakes, while on the rear staircase is the conductor and in the roadway are a CBT inspector and a depot mechanic. The little girl perched on the front steps next to her straw-boatered father looks to be around three years old. Behind the tram is the still fairly new Bournbrook Hotel, as well as some properties that were still under construction. (Whitcombe Collection)

CAR 108

Car 108 is seen in Bristol Road, Bournbrook at the Dawlish Road terminus in CBT ownership in around 1897. Despite the problems of battery operation, which included sluggish performance and leaking acid, the trams worked until replacement by conventional overhead electric cars on 14 May 1901. The batteries were carried behind the rocker panels, and what look like six smaller panels in the rocker panels of the tramcar were in reality the individual doors to the batteries. Dawlish Road depot continued to be used by CBT until they relinquished operation to Birmingham Corporation Tramways on 1 July 1911 whereupon the depot was transferred to the municipality. The Bristol Road tram service was operated by the largest fleet of battery accumulator trams in the country. These Falcon-built open-top bogie trams were very similar in design to the cable cars that operated on the Snow Hill–Handsworth line. The pioneering nature of this experimental service, although not without its critics at the time, must have been reasonably successful, as it lasted for nearly eleven years! (Whitcombe Collection)

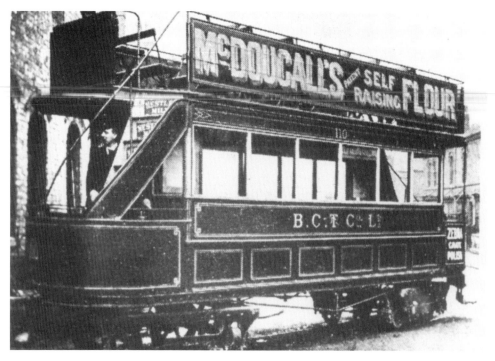

CAR 110

Turning into Bournbrook depot from Dawlish Road when in service with Birmingham Central Tramways is battery-powered accumulator car 110. The tram is in the second BCT livery of later crimson and pale cream, as it has the fleet number on the waist rail rather than within a garter on the lower side panels. This colour scheme was briefly carried over into CBT ownership after the takeover in October 1896. These battery-powered trams were quite large for the day; they were 28 feet 9 inches long and 6 feet wide, and with their batteries in position weighed around 9 tons. Yet they only had a single 15 hp motor driving both axles on one of the 4-foot-wheelbase bogies. The accumulator cars could be driven from either platform.

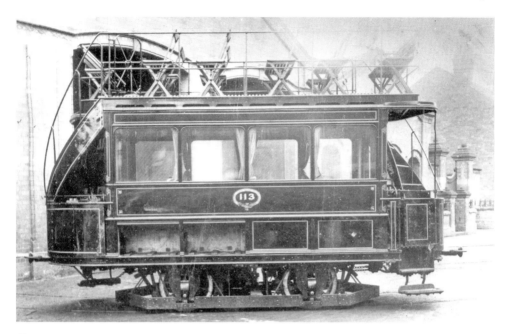

CAR 113

Seen on 25 June 1892 before it became BCT property is demonstration car 113, which entered service in May 1892. Again parked outside the entrance gates of Bournbrook depot in Dawlish Road, car 113 has its front two rocker panel doors open. This is where the batteries sat and were normally removed in the charging station. This tram double-deck open-top was built by Brown Marshall and had a seating capacity of only twenty-four with twenty on top and fourteen in the four side-windowed saloon. These four-wheelers had ECC electrics and were the first British-designed four-wheeled tram to be equipped with a separate motor-driven truck. The tramcar was only 19 feet 3 inches long with a 5-foot 3-inch wheelbase; it weighed 8½ tons and looked similar to a horse tram. Although the wheelbases were longer than the bogie cars, the very basic springing gave a very hard ride. Car 114 looked similar but smaller than 113 and was only 18 feet 4 inches long, weighing in at only 6 tons 12 cwt. It had General Electric Power electrics, which were also found on the North Metropolitan Tramway line on the Barking Road route, and had the older style of integral axle and motor. Neither of these two four-wheelers lasted a very long time, being delicensed for passenger service on 29 June 1894, but remaining in stock for a number of years despite their fleet numbers being reused as early as March 1895 on two new Falcon-manufactured cable trams.

CAR 104 (*Opposite below*)

Also standing the entrance to the BCT depot in Dawlish Road is car 104 in its original condition, with the fleet number on the side panel within a garter belt on a sage green and cream livery. It is in its original condition, as it still has curtains mounted in the saloon windows, which were quickly removed as they attracted dust. The card in the window is for the destination BOURNBROOK, though in truth they could only go to Birmingham or Suffolk Street. They did go to other destinations, however; after the conversion of the Bristol Road route to overhead operation by CBT, ever mindful of their financial problems, the accumulator cars were stripped of their motors and were apparently used as steam tram trailers, though being open top they would not have been popular with the passengers.

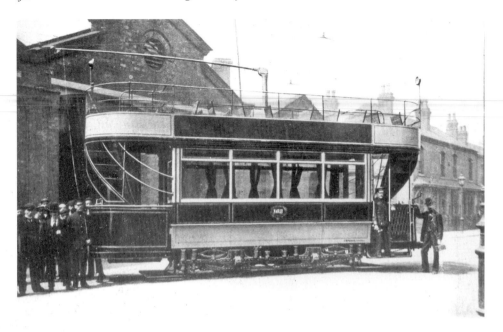

CBT 162

In 1901, just after the opening of the overhead electric tram route on 14 May 1901, CBT car 162 stands at the entrance to the Bournbrook depot in Dawlish Road. With bodies built by the Electric Railway & Tramway Carriage Works, these 37 hp trams could seat forty-eight passengers, but they were 27 feet 6 inches long and gave a smoother, faster journey than the preceding accumulator trams. Just beyond the depot is a row of late Victorian terraces which led to the nearby Bristol Road opposite the Bournbrook Hotel. Bournbrook depot was taken over by the Corporation on 1 July 1911 and it lasted as a Corporation tram depot until 11 July 1927 when Selly Oak depot was opened. Dawlish Road depot, when converted to electric operation, had a capacity for forty-six tramcars. The plan of the depot reveals its extent and layout.

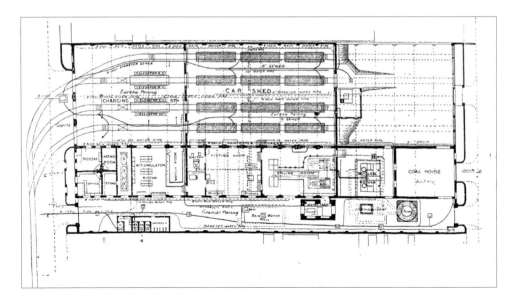

CARS 103 AND 104

The pair of battery elevators faced the entrance doors in Dawlish Road with on either side of these two roads there were to outer roads for trams to gain access to the storage rows which could each house three trams. The accumulator trams' lead-acid batteries were withdrawn from behind the rocker panels on trays and exchanged every day with recharged batteries; the clever replacement system from being on charge to being in the cradle on the tramcar only took around half an hour. An ingenious automatic electrical connection was made in the tram by the use of sprung brass clips connected to the car wiring. Each tram had a series of batteries consisting of ninety-six cells, which gave a current of around 192 volts. The recharging process, which charged the batteries up to their maximum capacity of 350 amps, took around ten hours. The Dawlish Road depot had these two charging gantries, onto which the trams were driven; the foundations of the gantries had foundations that were sunk down around 15 feet in order to support the recharging trams. The trams ran a sixteen-minute service, except for five days: on 30 January 1895 there was a severe fire in the accumulator room and the service was suspended until 4 February. Horse buses were substituted until repairs were completed and an initial twenty-minute service could be resumed. Cars 104 and 103 are in the charging station in Dawlish Road. The rocker panel doors on car 104 are open. A bank of cells is being raised by the left-hand lift to push into the side of 104, while on the other side of the car the lift is in its highest position with the top shelves empty. Technically, the arrangements at the Bournbrook charging station were often celebrated as being very good in the early days, being remarkably efficient at charging and replacing the heavy batteries. Just visible through the entrance behind the tram is the car shed with the associated inspection pits.

Dawlish Road Depot Frontage

By the early 1980s only the frontage of the former Birmingham Central Tramways Company depot in Dawlish Road, Bournville, was extant. The trams came from the distant Bristol Road on the left opposite the Bournbrook Hotel, and turned right into the middle three doors, with the track on the right having an extra line just inside the depot entrance. This is where the previous tramcars were posed although there are no known photographs of trams in Dawlish Road between the depot and Bristol Road.

CBT Car 168 in Bournbrook (*Opposite above*)

Leaving the former terminus of the accumulator tram service at Dawlish Road in Bristol Road, Bournbrook, in 1905 is CBT-built open-top tram 168, dating from 1902. It has travelled towards the new terminus from the top of the steep hill beyond Selly Oak railway bridge at Chapel Lane. The probable reason for the battery trams terminating at Dawlish Road was that they might not have been able to climb that gradient. The gabled shops on the left near to the junction with Grange Road, where the original 4-foot 8½-inch horse tram depot was located, date from the last decade of the nineteenth century. On the far corner of Grange Road is Jackson's furniture store. On the opposite side of Bristol Road is the three-storeyed eighteenth-century Bournbrook Tavern. On the right is Dawlish Road, where the CBT tramway depot was located. (Commercial postcard)

Car 112 (*Opposite below*)

The last of the twelve BCT accumulator battery trams was car 112, and it was used as the manufacturer's official photograph in 1890. Taken in Loughborough by the Falcon Company, the tram has yet to be fitted with lifeguards and canopy decency panels. Painted in BCT's sage green livery, if the operator's management had got its way, these could have been built as overhead electric trams. The BCT Company almost by default were moved towards the operation of battery trams, which were beset with technical difficulties that were frequently addressed but rarely successfully resolved.

16042   BRISTOL ROAD.   BOURNBROOK.

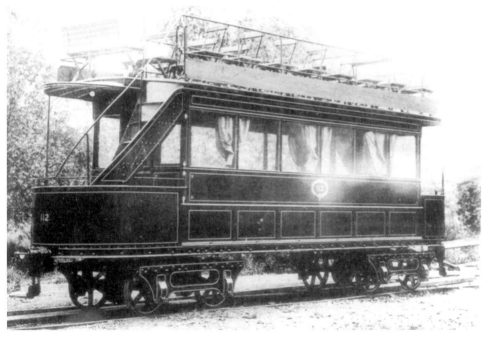

STEAM TRAMS IN OLD SQUARE AREA OF CENTRAL BIRMINGHAM

BIRMINGHAM & ASTON TRAMWAYS AND BIRMINGHAM CENTRAL TRAMWAYS SERVICES FROM OLD SQUARE TO CORPORATION STREET

Old Square was the first terminus in the town centre of Birmingham to use mechanical power to provide public transport. The first operator was the Birmingham & Aston Tramway Company, which began working to Witton on Boxing Day 1882 and opened its second line to Aston Cross and Salford Bridge on 23 February 1885. Shortly afterwards, thw first route operated by Birmingham Central Tramways began working to Perry Barr on 25 November 1884 and the Saltley via Gosta Green route began on 24 November 1885. These two routes were run as a through service between Perry Barr, Old Square and Saltley soon afterwards. There was also an unsuccessful service to Nechells via Gosta Green, which was opened on 29 March 1885, but the Nechells section was closed by November 1885 and replaced by horse trams, which terminated in Albert Street.

CBT Tram 61 and Trailer 74

Picking up passengers in Old Square around 1902 is CBT steam tram 61, which is working on the Perry Barr route. This was built by Kitson in 1899 and was one of their two-cylinder 'Improved' Standard type. It is pulling trailer 74, which was the last of the twenty bogie double-decker cars built in 1886 by Falcon. This tram seated thirty on each deck, those in the lower deck sitting in a seven side-windowed saloon, while those upstairs sat beneath a canopy top, which had closed ends that prevented the passengers from getting smuts from the steam locomotive. Behind the tram are the County Buildings, which were built in 1895. Opposite Old Square is the Grand Theatre, which, from its luxurious start as one of the premier theatres in Birmingham, declined to become a music hall. With dwindling patrons in the late 1920s and early 1930s, but the end came when the theatre closed on 13 May 1933. Finally it reopened as the Grand Casino Dance Hall. It was closed again a few years later and was finally demolished in the 1960s when the area was redeveloped as part of the Priory Ringway redevelopment scheme. (Whybrow Collection)

Old Square (*Opposite below*)

The problem with steam tram operations beginning in Old Square is that it was operated for many years by two distinct operators, the Birmingham & Aston Tramways Co. and the Birmingham Central Company, who later became the City of Birmingham Tramways Company. In 1902, a Birmingham & Aston steam tram has arrived in Old Square and is unloading passengers opposite the Minories. This passageway had been created around 1700 to link Old Square to Bull Street, and its name commemorates the friars minor of the former St Thomas's Priory, which stood on this site and gave its name to the streets Upper and Lower Priory. The Augustinian Priory Hospital of St Thomas the Apostle was a monastery endowed by wealthy Birmingham merchants before 1286. It had extensive lands in Birmingham, Aston and Saltley, whose rents helped pay for the care of the poor and the sick. This priory, along with thousands of others across the country, was dissolved by Henry VIII in 1536. The tram, having unloaded, will turn in a wide U-shaped loop to draw up on the opposite side of the square in order to load up again with more passengers. (Commercial postcard)

BCT Tram 11 with Trailer 18

Standing in Old Square, still with the garter-surrounded fleet number, is a Birmingham Central steam tram locomotive and trailer, which is working on the Perry Barr service. This was the original tram track layout in Old Square; it ended in a single siding once the Corporation Street curves into the square had been negotiated. This resulted in a good deal of manoeuvring and so the layout was changed during 1900 to the more easily workable loop around Old Square. The eastern side of Old Square's Georgian buildings had already been demolished along with the former headquarters of the Birmingham Central Tramways Ltd, which stood on the left. This would date the tram being in Old Square in 1896 not long before a new company, the City of Birmingham Tramways Co. Ltd, was formed on 29 September 1896 out of the financial ashes of the former BCT operation. The steam tram is number 14, a standard two-cylinder Kitson locomotive, built in 1884 and lasting until the end of steam operation in the City on 31 December 1906. The six side-windowed bogie trailer had a seating split of twenty-eight/twenty-six. Car 18, which also dated from 1884, was constructed by Falcon with a canopy top and enclosed ends to the upper deck. (Newman University)

OLD SQUARE

Working on the Perry Barr route is a Birmingham Central Tramways Kitson locomotive pulling a Falcon trailer. The tram is about to leave Old Square in around 1890 and is standing in the original single line layout in the stub terminus in the middle of the square. The advertisement on the decency panel between the decks of the trailer is for the beers of George Taylor who was established at the Hockley Brewery and who closed down between 1890 and 1892. The tram is facing Corporation Street and overlooking Old Square is the New Theatre. The theatre, described as the 'Drury Lane of the Midlands', was designed by W. H. Ward and opened on 14 November 1883. The theatre was renamed 'The Grand' soon after it opened and had seating for 2,200 people. The interior of the theatre was redesigned in 1907 at a cost of 0,000. It reopened as a music hall owned by the Moss Empires group, and stars of the time, such as W. C. Fields, Marie Lloyd and Vesta Tilley, appeared at the theatre.

Old Square and Upper Priory

Old Square was used by both the Birmingham & Aston Tramways Company and the Birmingham Central Tramways Company. The B&A service went to Witton via Aston Cross and from Aston Cross to Salford Bridge, while BCT operated services to Perry Barr and to Saltley via Gosta Green. The first route to open was the B&A service to Witton on Boxing Day 1882, while the last route to open from Old Square was on 29 March 1885. Prior to the construction of Corporation Street, Old Square was a quiet space surrounded by early Georgian houses. Newbury's Department Store was owned by Charles Newbury who after being apprenticed to the Hudson's Dry Soap company, who were based in nearby West Bromwich, set up his goods warehouse in Old Square. He later turned his shop into a 'great bargain emporium' using the slogan 'THE WORLD'S TRADERS' on their advertising. The road beyond the trams and Newbury's store is Upper Priory, which led to Steelhouse Lane. The CBT steam trams are bound for Perry Barr via Newtown Row and survived on this route until the expiry of their operating lease on New Year's Eve 1906, after which date they were replaced by Corporation electric trams. The tram standing in front of Newbury's carries a large advertisement for Ogden's Guinea-Gold cigarettes. Ogdens were based in Liverpool and in later years they were better known for St Bruno pipe tobacco. (Whybrow Collection)

Old Square B&A (*Opposite above*)

The complete view into Old Square shows the Wesleyan & General Assurance building on the right and the Jevons & Mellors shop between Corporation Street and the Minories on the left. The sheer size of the Newbury's Department Store can be appreciated, especially as it dwarfs the double-decker steam trams. The layout of the steam tram tracks formed a loop around Old Square, which allowed for kerbside unloading and loading of passengers. The tram on the right facing Corporation Street is Birmingham & Aston steam tram locomotive No. 1, built by Kitson in 1882 and taken over by CBT at the beginning of 1904. The CBT tram and trailer at the far end of Old Square are working on their service to Saltley but will have to wait until the Aston-bound B&A tram moves off and into Corporation Street. (Whitcombe Collection)

OLD SQUARE AND CORPORATION STREET

As a steam tram enters Old Square from Corporation Street, a Birmingham & Aston steam tram leaves on its journey to Aston. The railings around the subterranean gentlemen's lavatories act as an early traffic island in the middle of Old Square, around which the steam trams negotiated the entrance and exit to the track on the square. The large store on the corner of Corporation Street and Old Square was built in 1883 to the design of Kirk & Jones and was occupied by Jevons & Mellors, a gentleman's hosiers; it is separated from Newbury's store by the Minories. This building was constructed on the site of Berlin House on the corner of Old Square as part of the second phase of the extension of Corporation Street. (Commercial postcard)

Inbound Tram in Corporation Street

Coming into Birmingham from Saltley is a CBT tram that has just passed where the track leaving Old Square enters Corporation Street. The tram is coming from Perry Barr, Aston or Saltley, and, once beyond the railings around the underground toilets, would turn right into Old Square where they would unload their passengers. On the right is the Grand Theatre, while the shops on the left with their sunblinds down are below the Wesleyan & General Assurance building built in 1896. The distant tower in Corporation Street belongs to the Methodist Central Hall, which was opened in 1903. (Commercial postcard)

Corporation Street at Newton Street (*Opposite above*)

A distant steam tram and trailer are about to pass the junction on the left with Newton Street as it travels out of the City along Corporation Street. The tower of the Methodist Central Hall is directly opposite the Victoria Law Courts. Queen Victoria laid the foundation stone on 20 March 1887 as Birmingham's contribution to her Golden Jubilee year. The Victoria Law Courts, designed by Sir Aston Webb, who had been responsible for the new façade of Buckingham Palace, were opened in 1891 and represented the last flowering of the Joseph Chamberlain ethos of civic development in Birmingham. The French-style, red-brick, terracotta construction dominated the last gasp of the development of 'Civic Pride' in Corporation Street, which had 'run out of steam' by the last decade of the nineteenth century. (Commercial postcard)

Near Victoria Law Courts

When the weather was hot, the drivers of the steam trams must have had a very difficult task, being in a fairly confined space with a hot firebox, steam and boiling water to contend with. In order to cool down, the driver often opened the front cab door of the enclosed tram bodywork in order to get a cooler draught into his cab. This is precisely what the driver of this CBT steam locomotive has done. The tram is in Corporation Street just to the north of the Victoria Law Courts and appears to be working on the route from Perry Barr.

BIRMINGHAM & ASTON TRAMWAYS COMPANY

STEAM LOCOS

Fleet No.	Manufacturer	Type	Years	Withdrawn
1–6	Kitson		12/1882 – 3/1883	To Aston Manor UDC 25/3/1903
7–8	Wilkinson	Vertical boiler 2 cyl 7 in. x 9 in.	12/1882 – 1887	
9–12	Kitson		9/1883 – 12/1883	To Aston Manor UDC 25/3/1903
13–27	Kitson Heavy	Some built as 2 cyl compounds	1/1885 – 10/1886	To Aston Manor UDC 25/3/1903

STEAM TRAM TRAILERS

Fleet No.	Manufacturer	Type		Years	
1–10	Metropolitan	Open top single truck. 6–10 rebuilt 1896–99 as balcony bogie cars	24/20	12/1882	To Aston Manor UDC 25/3/1903
11–18	Starbuck	Balcony bogie car	62 seats	7/1883	To Aston Manor UDC 25/3/1903
19–22	Metropolitan RCW	Balcony bogie car	60 seats	1885	To Aston Manor UDC 25/3/1903
23–26	Starbuck	Balcony bogie car	62 seats	1886	To Aston Manor UDC 25/3/1903

The Birmingham & Aston Tramways Company was the first steam tram operator to operate in Birmingham; its first line from Old Square to Witton opened on 26 December 1882, followed by the line to Aston Cross and Salford Bridge line, which opened 23 February 1885, although double-deck trams could not pass beneath Aston station bridge. The company had 3 miles and 66 chains of track in Aston, and other 1 mile 2 chains across the boundary in Birmingham, making a total of 4 miles and 1,496 yards of track.

The twenty-one-year lease was due to expire on 31 December 1903, but negotiations with the newly formed Aston UDC led to the local council briefly becoming a steam tram operator. It was taken over on 1 January 1904 by CBT just three days before Birmingham Corporation Tramways began operating its first electric service from Steelhouse Lane to Aston Brook Street, which was the boundary with Aston Manor UDC. All the former B&A steam tram routes were converted to electric operation in stages by CBT, and this was completed on 14 November 1904 when the Aston Cross–Gravelly Hill route was converted. This route was briefly operated by single-deck electric tramcars until Aston Station railway bridge was replaced by a new girder construction on Sunday 25 March 1906, which allowed double-deck trams to pass beneath the railway line.

CORPORATION STREET TO ASTON CROSS

CORPORATION STREET AT OLD SQUARE

B&A steam tram 23 has come into the City in Corporation Street and has just entered the stub line beyond the reverse track curve into Old Square. The tram's position shows how the trams got in and out of Old Square. Car 23, built by Kitson in 1885, has to draw forward so that the trailer was beyond the points. The tram would reverse into Old Square up to the stub terminus and then leave by taking the left arm, which would take it on to the outbound line in Corporation Street, just beyond the enclosed four-wheel horse-drawn Brougham carriage. Two CBT steam trams are travelling out of the city, with the distant one about to pass the Victoria Law Courts.

VICTORIA LAW COURTS

The Victoria Law Courts is the most important building in Corporation Street and is the only one to be Grade 1 listed. The granting of an Assize to the town was dependent on the provision of suitable courts. A competition for the design of the Law Court building showing off Birmingham's civic pride took place, and was in 1886 won by Sir Aston Webb and Ingress Bell, who were two London architects. The Jacobean-style building was constructed between 1887 and 1891 with the main façade almost symmetrical about the entrance porch, with two storeys and gables to the high pitched roof and with two tiers of mullioned windows, and was faced externally in red brick and red terracotta. A B&A steam tram climbs up Corporation Street from Aston Street as it makes its way towards Old Square. The tram is passing the newly built Victoria Law Courts before the 1892 extension was constructed on the corner of Newton Street on the left.

CBT ELECTRIC TRAM 205

On 16 June 1904, Birmingham Corporation extended its new electric tram service from Steelhouse Lane across the Aston UDC boundary from Aston Brook Street to Aston Cross. Meanwhile, the CBT line via Aston Cross and Witton had also been converted to electric operation, and until Witton depot was free of its steam trams, trailers and the steam tram infrastructure, the new CBT electric trams were operated from Miller Street for two weeks until the depot in Witton Lane was wired. On 16 September 1904, the first CBT electric car to test the new welded electric tram tracks on the Witton route was driven along Aston Road North towards the distant Aston Cross. Car 205, a Brush–bodied forty-eight-seat open-top electric tram, mounted on Brush type 8-foot-wheelbase, four-wheel trucks and dating from early 1904, is acting as the first test tramcar to negotiate the new trackwork, although it does appear to have a lot of passengers in the lower saloon. It is painted in CBT's crimson and cream livery and actually carried the coat of arms of Aston Manor UDC on the sides, even though they were owned by the Company. In the foreground are the much worn steam tram tracks, which were lighter than the replacement electric tram tracks and were not welded, making traversing them using an electric tram extremely dangerous. Hidden by the traction pole on the left are two of the former B&A steam trams, making this scene really *'out with the old and in with the new'* as CBT replaced the steam trams just three days later. (W. Gratwicke)

Aston Cross *c.* 1889

The old clock at Aston Cross was erected in 1854 to replace the medieval preaching cross that stood at the junction of Lichfield Road with Park Lane and Rocky Lane. The new structure was a brick-built tower that was three storeys high, designed to resemble the Jacobean style of the nearby Aston Hall. By 1891 the tower had become unstable and the clock unreliable, and so it was demolished and replaced. In that year a new Aston Cross Clock, set in a square cast-iron tower with the Aston Board's coat-of-arms and a plaque on it, was given by Lewis Richards, the Chairman of Aston Board. A couple of years before the rather ungainly brick clock tower was demolished, a steam tram is about to make its way along Lichfield Road towards Salford Bridge on the Birmingham & Aston Tramways service, which had opened on 23 February 1885. The buildings on the left at the bottom of Park Road date from the 1840s, while those behind the waiting horse cabs were demolished, to be replaced by the new art-deco-style Ansells Brewery, opened in the mid-1930s. (Commercial postcard)

Aston Cross *c.* 1904 (*Opposite above*)

By around early 1904, Aston Cross had not substantially changed, although the impressive clock had replaced the previous ungainly mid-Victorian brick structure. The B&A double-deck bogie trailer tram in the foreground appears to be parked, as it is not attached to a steam tram locomotive. To its right is Aston Cross Library with its tall Dutch-style gable. This was opened on 30 October 1903, which dates this view between then and September 1904, when the steam tram services were replaced by electric tramcars. The distant tram in Lichfield Road has just left the tram stop at Aston Cross, adjacent to the still fairly new cast-iron clock, and is on its way to Salford Bridge. The tram tracks going up the hill to the left of the junction are those to Witton Square, and the tramcar sheds in Witton Lane, though en route these trams would pass Aston Hall, the medieval Aston Parish Church and Aston Villa's then almost new Villa Park football stadium. (C. Carter)

BIRMINGHAM CORPORATION TRAM 543

The former LNWR railway bridge across Lichfield Road at Aston was rebuilt over the weekend that ended on Sunday 25 March 1906 to accommodate, initially, CBT's open-top electric double-deck cars. The original bridge had initially prevented the Birmingham & Aston Company from operating double-deck steam trams from under the bridge to Gravelly Hill, but this was soon remedied by the use of a single-deck trailer operating the through service, though it is surmised that this was only operated from Aston Cross with double-deck cars stopping just short of Aston station bridge. On 25 April, just over two months before the final Birmingham Corporation tram abandonment, UEC-bodied bogie car 543, built in 1913, approaches the bridge when working on the 2 route to Erdington. (R. J. S. Wiseman)

ASTON CROSS TO WITTON

PARK ROAD

On leaving Aston Cross on the way to Witton, the steam trams climbed Park Road, crossed Victoria Road and descended the steep hill towards Aston Parish Church before turning into Witton Lane. A Birmingham Corporation Brush-bodied bogie car from the 587 Class comes down the hill in 1949 when working on the 3X route. Park Road itself was a strange contrast, with Victorian terraces on the one side, but to the right the passengers could look out over the magnificent Jacobean Aston Hall and its surrounding park. The house was built by the Holte family who were the landowners in Aston, between April 1618 and April 1635. (R. T. Wilson)

LOCO 13 (*Opposite above*)

Birmingham & Aston steam tram No. 13 Kitson locomotive entered service in January 1885 and was virtually brand new when it was parked on the curve into Church Lane from Park Road, Aston. It was the first of fifteen locomotives that entered service in time for the opening of the company's second line to Gravelly Hill on 23 February of that year. Behind the tram is the junction of Trinity Road and Witton Lane before the Jacobean-styled Holte Hotel was built in the late nineteenth century when the Holte End stand was first used as an open terrace for Aston Villa's 1897 soccer season. This area was part of the Aston Lower Grounds, built around the ornamental duck pond in the grounds of Aston Hall, which had a menagerie, laid-out gardens and many other entertainment features, including regular fairground attractions. Unlike the nearby Birmingham Central Tramways, the B&A's steam locomotives frequently carried advertisements on their side panels such as those on loco 13 for Bryant & May Matches and Sunlight Soap.

LOCO 7 WITH TRAILER 1

The Birmingham & Aston Tramway Company purchased two steam tram locomotives from William Wilkinson of Wigan around the turn of 1882 and 1883. These were numbered 7 and 8, and at £750 each were some £75 more expensive than the previous Kitson steam trams. They had vertical boilers and could easily be distinguished, as their chimneys were in the centre of the tram's enclosed bodywork rather than the more normal end position. They were underpowered and were not used after 1887. It is pulling the first of the ten MRCW four-wheel trailers that were briefly used in pairs until the Board of Trade banned this practice. These quaint, if ungainly, trailers had knife-board seating in the upper saloon as well as a single protective end canopy to stop the emissions from the steam tram covering the passengers.

LOCO 21 WITH TRAILER 21

The construction of this Metropolitan RCW-bodied trailer of 1885 was typical of this genre. Carrying some sixty passengers on a 30-foot-long chassis, the plate-frame bogies were placed at the extreme ends of the car in order to reduce the risk of overturning due to the sideways pull of the two cylinder engines' drawbars, especially noticeable on the curves. It was not for nothing that steam trams in Birmingham were nicknamed 'shufflers'. Trailer 21 has a full-length canopy with open sides, but with end screens that protected the upper saloon passengers from the smoke and smuts emitted from the locomotive's chimney. These trailer cars had a capacity of sixty seated passengers, and the circulating landings to reach the 'knifeboard' seating on the upper deck were inside the end screens. The locomotive is 21, another of the longer Kitson 'Five-panel' trams that were longer than the earlier Kitson models, and allowed more space inside the enclosed bodywork for the driver, as well as allowing for more coke bags to be carried on the footplate.

Loco 19

Ready to begin another journey to Birmingham is five-panelled Kitson engine 19. On the inward journey, the steam trams went into Witton Lane then forked left between Aston Park and the Lower Grounds site, later to become Villa Park, and in to Trinity Road. At Bevington Road the trams turned right through an area of 1870s-built terraced housing before reaching Witton Road. The B&A then joined the tracks from Lozells of the BCT Company, after which they both reached Witton Square. The B&A trams then turned right to terminate in front of Witton tram depot, thus completing a somewhat long loop around the backstreets of Witton. On the roof of the steam locomotive are the condensers that converted any steam back into water, thus preventing steam, and to some extent smoke, from escaping into the atmosphere. The same method of condensing gear was used on the steam locomotives used on the first underground railway in the World in London, when the Metropolitan Railway opened its lines between Bishops Road, Paddington and Farringdon on 10 January 1863. By July 1864, the Metropolitan used steam locomotives with exhaust condensers built by Beyer Peacock of Manchester for tunnel working; this became the standard for both the Metropolitan and District Railways. Just hidden by the rebuilt MRCW single-ended bogie trailer is the B&A's Witton tram depot, outside which is parked another steam tram and trailer. When Aston Villa were playing at home, the steam trams waited at this terminus point to pick up passengers and also stopped again, if there was room for any more passengers, just beyond the Holte End open terracing.

Steam Tram 6 (*Opposite below*)

Standing in Witton Lane outside the Birmingham & Aston Company's tram depot is Kitson engine. The engine is virtually brand new, having entered service in December 1882 when the first steam trams to operate in Birmingham began operation on Boxing Day of that year. The four-wheel, open-top trailers were built by Metropolitan RCW as the first passenger-carrying trailers; these were numbered 1–10 in the B&A fleet. By July 1883 the company had virtually been obliged to purchase eight new, large top-covered balcony bogie trams from Starbuck of Birkenhead, as the Board of Trade stopped the intended operation of these four-wheeled trailers coupled together in pairs as seen here. (D. Gladwin)

Loco 14

Standing outside Witton depot, facing away from Witton Square, is steam tram locomotive 14. This is another one of the Kitson engines built in 1885. It and the surrounding houses are decorated with flags and bunting, though at this distance in time it is impossible to say what the event actually was, though it might have been the Coronation of King Edward VII on 9 August 1902. The tram and trailer have worked to the Lower Grounds on a shortworking. The conductor on the right, as per normal, is smartly dressed, but the poor driver in his overalls is covered with coal dust, oil and grime, showing what a hard job it was to drive a steam tram.

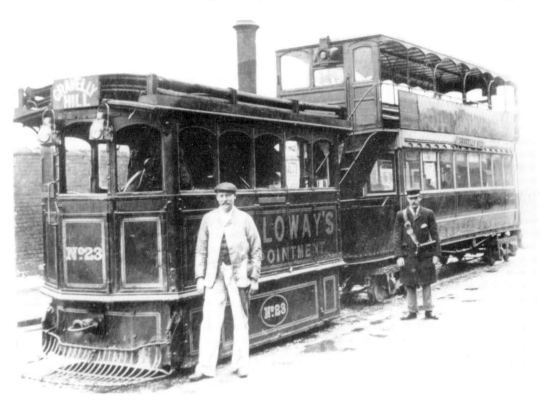

Loco 23

Another one of the fifteen B&A five-panel Kitson steam locomotives and its top-covered bogie trailer; it could either be parked in Witton Lane or, as the destination slip board shows GRAVELLY HILL, at that terminus in Lichfield Road. It is probable that it is at the former as the driver's dungarees and jacket are still clean! Unfortunately the background has largely been washed out save for the brick wall to the left of the locomotive.

2489 (JOJ 489)

Witton tram shed was built in 1882 and was opened on 26 December 1882 to house the steam trams that first operated a public service between the Old Square and Witton. The main shed still survives, with its inscription, 'BOROUGH OF ASTON MANOR TRAMWAYS DEPOT', and four arched entrances and tracks dividing into seven dividing inside the hall. To the left of the main shed was the locomotive shed, entered off the road by a single track.

By 16 June 1904, electric Corporation trams ran through to Aston Cross, where the connecting steam trams had to reverse. By 19 September 1904, Company electric trams, temporarily housed in the Miller Street Corporation tram depot, only ran through to Aston Church while the depot was being electrified. CBT trams ran through from Steelhouse Lane to Witton on 6 October 1904. The second former B&A route to Salford Bridge was electrified on 14 November 1904. After closure on 30 September 1950, it was used to break up some 129 trams made redundant by the closure of the Bristol Road and Cotteridge routes on 5 July 1952. It then became a dormy shed to house thirty trams while Miller Street was being converted, and after further scrapping of trams during July and August it was eventually closed by 1955, whereupon it became a car showroom. Eventually it became the Aston Manor Transport Museum, and on 11 March 2007, the author's former Birmingham City Transport bus 2489, (JOJ 489), a 1950 Crossley DD42/6 with a Crossley H30/24R body, is seen above standing outside the former tram depot before heading off on the 25-mile round trip around the 11 Outer Circle bus route from the museum. (D. R. Harvey)

BIRMINGHAM CENTRAL TRAMWAYS/ CITY OF BIRMINGHAM TRAMWAYS COMPANY TRAMCAR FLEET

Horse-Drawn Cars

Fleet No.	Manufacturer	Type	Seating	Origin	Years
1-10	Falcon	Double-deck Open-top	20/18	BCT 1896	1884–1906
?	various	various		BTO	1876–1886

Steam Locos

Locos 85, 86, 89, 90, 96 and 97 were retained for shunting cable cars until 1911.

1–14	Kitson	Standard 2 cyl 8½ in. x 12 in.	BCT 1896	1884–1907
15–26	Kitson	Standard 2 cyl 8½ in. x12 in.	BCT 1896	1885–1907
27	Falcon	Built as 4cyl compound. Later rebuilt as a Standard 2 cyl 8 in. x 14 in.	BCT 1896	1885–1907
27–34	Falcon	Standard Scott Russell 2 cyl 8 in. x 14 in.	BCT 1896	1885–1907
35–36	Kitson	Standard 2 cyl 8½ in. x 12 in.	BCT 1896	1885–1907
37–50	Falcon	Standard Scott Russell 2 cyl 8 in. x 14 in.	BCT 1896	1885–1907
51–56	Falcon	Standard Scott Russell 2 cyl 8 in. x 14 in.	BCT 1896	1886–1907
57	Falcon	2 cyl compound 8 in. x 14 in.	BCT 1896	1886–1907
58–70	Beyer Peacock	'Locomotive type' 2 cyl 8½ in. x 14 in.	BCT 1886	1886–1907, 60–62 withdrawn 1898
71	Burrell	2 cyl compound 10 in. x 14 in.		1886–1886
71–72	Kitson	Standard 'Improved' 2 cyl 8½ in. x 12 in.	BCT 1896	1893–1907
73–82	Kitson	Standard 'Improved' 2 cyl 8½ in. x 12 in.	BCT 1896	1894–1907
83–90	Kitson	Standard 'Improved' 2 cyl 8½ in. x 12 in.		1898–1907
57/ 60	Kitson	Standard 'Improved' 2 cyl 8½ in. x 12 in.		1898–1907
61–62	Kitson	Standard 'Improved' 2 cyl 8½ in. x 12 in.		1899–1907
91–92	Kitson	Standard 2 cyl 8½ in. x 12 in.	Birmingham & Aston, (1903)	1886–1907
93	Birmingham & Midland Tramways	Standard 2 cyl 8½ in. x 12 in.	Birmingham & Midland Tramways 13, (1904)	1899–1907
94–95	Kitson	Standard 2 cyl 8½ in. x 12 in.	Birmingham & Midland Tramways 29–30, (1904)	1896/1895–1907
96–97	Birmingham &	Standard 2 cyl 8½	Birmingham &	1899/1900–1907

STEAM TRAM TRAILER CARS

11–23	Falcon	Double-deck 6 side windows Canopy-top bogie	28/26	BCT 1896	1884–1907
24–45	Falcon	Double-deck 6 side windows Canopy-top bogie	28/26	BCT 1896	1885–1907
46–54	Falcon	Double-deck 7 side windows Canopy-top bogie	30/30	BCT 1896	1885–1907
55–74	Falcon	Double-deck 7 side windows Canopy-top bogie	30/30	BCT 1896	1886–1907
125–130	Midland RCW	Double-deck single ended 9 side windows Canopy-top bogie	34/36		1899–1907
131–136 137–140 *were never built*	CBT	Double-deck single-ended 9 side window Canopy-top bogie	34/36		1900–1907

The Birmingham Central Tramways Co. Ltd (BCT) and its successor the City of Birmingham Tramways Co. Ltd (CBT) operated a total of 17 miles and 1,342 yards. This made the system the third largest in the UK after the 4-foot 7½-inch gauge, 23½ mile one in Huddersfield and the nearby South Staffordshire System at 22 miles and 1,122 yards also on the 3-foot 6-inch gauge.

BCT/CBT Route to Perry Barr

The BCT steam tram service from Old Square via Newtown Row, Six Ways and Birchfield Road to Perry Barr opened on 25 November 1884 and remained operating until its lease expired, whereupon it closed on 31 December 1906. This route was opened with Corporation electric tramcars from Martineau Street to Newtown Row on 1 January 1907 and was extended to Chain Walk, just beyond Six Ways, Aston, on 23 April 1907. Due to legal problems with working across the boundary with Handsworth UDC, the through service to Perry Barr was not opened until 8 December 1909.

NEWTOWN ROW

On the right, on the corner of St Stephen's Street, is St Stephen's Church, built in an Early English style in brick and sandstone, and consecrated in 1844, becoming the centre of religious life in the Newtown area for over a century. Travelling northwards along Newtown Row towards Perry Barr is a City of Birmingham Tramway's steam tram and trailer. Nicknamed 'shufflers' because of the shuffling gait along the track caused by the pushing of their outside cylinders, the steam tram is a much maligned beast, as it brought the first reliable public transport to a lot of people in the late nineteenth century. Some of the worst housing in the Victorian Birmingham area lay between the north–south roads of Summer Lane and Newtown Row in the area to the left of the steam tram. On the south side of nearby Lower Tower Street, houses were back-to-backs around a courtyard. Some back-to-backs had two rooms on each floor, but the smaller types had only 'one up and one down', with maybe an attic in the roof space for the children's bedroom. None had proper sanitation or running water, and they shared an earth closet and a cold water tap with all the other houses in their courtyard.

irton's Arms, Aston.

BARTON'S ARMS

The Barton's Arms is located between High Street, Newtown and Potters Lane. The CBT steam tram is climbing towards Six Ways, Aston, on its way to Perry Barr. The pub dates from 1901 and was designed by the local Midland pub architectural company of James & Lister Lea for Mitchells & Butlers. This magnificent pub still exists with its stained- and etched-glass windows, while the interior has walls lined with Minton tiles and wooden and glass snob screens. It was frequented by the many great artistes, such as Gracie Fields, Will Hay, George Robey and Stan Laurel and Oliver Hardy, who played at the nearby Aston Hippodrome. (Commercial postcard)

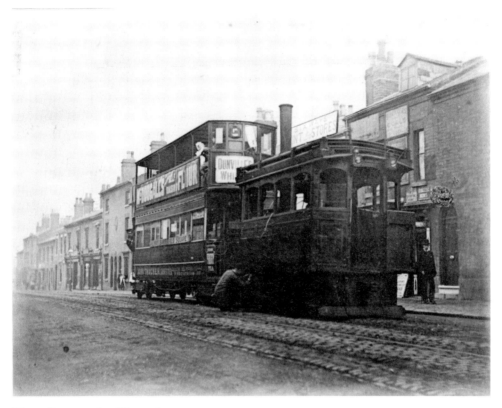

HIGH STREET, SIX WAYS, ASTON

A CBT Kitson tram locomotive stands in High Street, Six Ways, just short of the Alma Street and Lozells Road junction, where it would cross the CBT Lozells steam tram service. At the rear of the double-deck trailer, the tram's conductor looks on anxiously as the tram driver makes some mechanical adjustment. The tram displays the route letter P for Perry Barr; all the tram routes were given letters, but because of the levels of illiteracy at the time, the route letters and the background on which the destination letter was printed were given different colours so it didn't matter if you couldn't read. The stencil for the Perry Barr route was on a black background. This was the oldest part of Aston's Newtown, and the houses and tenements behind the tram looking back to Whitehead Road are some of the earliest, dating from the 1850s. Alongside the tram is the Six Ways Stores and at the front of the tram is a newsagent and tobacconist's shop where there is a news hoarding. This has written on it the headline 'Japan's terms of peace', which dates it to around the last couple of days of August 1905, when the victorious Japanese agreed terms with the Russians after their defeat in the Russo-Japanese War.

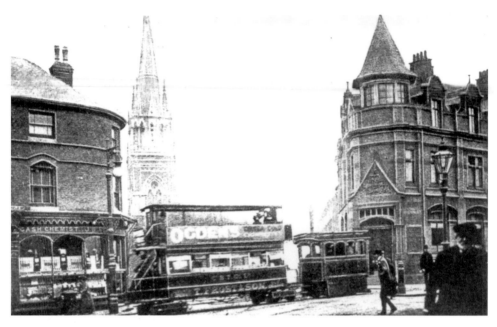

SIX WAYS, ASTON

The steam tram service through Newtown was the first to be operated by CBT, and ran between Old Square in the town centre and Perry Barr just beyond the Birchfield Road depot at the junction with Witton Lane. The route to Perry Barr was opened on 25 November 1884 and was linked to the Saltley route. Thus this steam tram and trailer has a SALTLEY destination slip board below the lower saloon windows as it works into Old Square and then out of town by way of Gosta Green, Great Lister Street, to the terminus just short of Saltley Viaduct. Both services continued until 31 December 1906 when the CBT lease expired, and the routes were taken over by the municipality on the following day. On conversion to an electric tramway, the Corporation only went as far as Newtown Row, as legal disputes prevented a through service to Perry Barr (this did not begin until 8 December 1909). Standing at Six Ways, Aston, with Victoria Road beyond the steam tram locomotive, the tram is on its way to Newtown and Birmingham. Behind the tram, between Gash's chemist shop and Christ Church Baptist Chapel, is the entrance to Witton Road on the left. The church had been built in the 1860s, and after many years of dereliction is now fitted out as luxury flats. (Commercial postcard)

BIRCHFIELD ROAD (*Opposite above*)

A CBT steam tram and trailer climb the hill in Birchfield Road from Perry Barr in around 1902. It is displaying the destination letter P in the front upper-saloon window as it makes its way towards Trinity Road and then onward to Six Ways, Aston. The invasion of cyclists coasting down the hill towards Perry Barr is avoiding the tram tracks and the tram as it trundles towards them. Birchfield Road was a comparatively well-to-do area, and behind the elaborate gateposts, walls and mature trees were large, detached mid-nineteenth-century villas. This is further borne out by the rather smart open carriage on the right. These villas tended to be owned by people engaged in managing and owning businesses in Birmingham. (Progress)

LOCOMOTIVE 5

One of the original BCT 1-14 Class of Kitson Standard two-cylinder steam tram locomotives of 1884 stands in Birchfield Road in the summer of the following year. It is working on the Perry Barr service. The style of the morning coat being worn by the conductor standing in the road between the locomotive and the trailer was redolent of the previous decade. The trailer is one of the 1885 Falcon double-deck, seven side-windowed, canopy-top bogie trams and is carrying an advertisement for Keen's mustard. This London-based company merged with Robinsons, a barley merchant, in 1862 before being taken over by Colman's of Norwich in 1903. As per usual the tram is running firebox first with the chimney nearest to the trailer.

CBT LOCOMOTIVE 11 AND TRAILER 14

Although this steam tram combination is parked in almost the same place as those in the previous photograph, the important feature is that the trailer car is carrying the side slip board SALTLEY | OLD SQUARE and the letter S in the upper-saloon destination box. The mountings for the slip boards show that they could easily be lifted out as they were reversible; in this case the far board had PERRY BARR on the reverse side. Steam tram 11 is another of the Kitson Standard two-cylinder locomotives of 1884 and it is hauling trailer 14, a Falcon fifty-four-seater, double-deck, six side-windowed canopy bogie car also dating from 1884. Unusually the photographer has captured the wisp of smoke escaping from the chimney of the tram.

BCT PERRY BARR DEPOT

BCT's Perry Barr steam tram depot was located in Birchfield Road between Wilmore Road and Wellington Road and was directly opposite the Perry Barr Institute. It opened in time for the commencement of the steam tram service from Old Square to Perry Barr on 25 November 1884. Birchfield Road was acquired by BCT on the closure of the Perry Barr steam tram service and was reopened on 2 May 1907 as an electrified tram depot with a capacity for around twenty trams, used as mainly peak-hour extras on the Perry Barr service to duplicate workings from Miller Street and to provide extras on Villa Park Specials. It was finally closed for trams on 3 October 1924 and reopened as a bus garage on 28 October the following year. Perry Barr was a six-road depot and had a covered, brick-built car shed. Just one year after opening, the trailer cars were being stored in the three roads that were under cover. The depot operated three steam tram routes with each one displaying a different route letter. N was for Nechells, which was very short-lived route only operating from March to November 1885 before being replaced by the BCT horse tram service. The second route had the destination letter P for Perry Barr, while the A service for Aston was carried by Kitson locomotive No. 16's trailer. The steam trams were stored in the open three roads to the left of the carriage shed, and the allocation of locomotives were generally those constructed by Kitson of Leeds.

399 (OG 399)

Towards the end of 1950, all of the surviving re-bodied 7.4-litre petrol-engine AEC 'Regent' 661s had congregated at Birchfield Road garage as this was the last garage to have petrol tanks and pumps, and was regarded as the 'home of geriatric buses'. In the 1920s and 30s Birchfield Road garage was opened and closed no less than three times but became a permanent overspill garage on 18 November 1940 for Perry Barr and remained in use until it was finally closed on 20 August 1966. Parked on the forecourt of Birchfield Road garage on 5 October 1950 is 399, (OG 399), an MoS-style Brush re-bodied petrol-engine AEC 'Regent' 661s. 399's chassis dated from 1930, but was deemed good enough to be re-bodied by Brush, re-entering service in 1943 with a straight staircase H30/21R body. The old Birmingham Central Tramways depot buildings had long been demolished except for the single-storey office block on the right, which was a remnant of the transport being provided from this site some sixty-six years earlier.

PERRY BARR

Looking towards the distant Perry Barr terminus just short of the railway station of the BCT steam tram route is a Kitson locomotive and an early Falcon trailer. The Grand Junction railway station was opened in 1837 and this paved the way for the development of a Victorian village between the station and Aston Lane in what was then the Parish of Handsworth. This road junction at Aston Lane is beneath the tower on the skyline and led to Witton Square and Villa Park, home of Aston Villa FC. The date is around 1905 and the CBT lease for operating steam trams is shortly due for renewal. The little boy on the pavement to the left of the tram is wearing a sailor suit popularised by Queen Victoria's decision in 1846 to dress the four-year-old Prince of Wales, Albert Edward, in a scaled-down version of the sailor suit. By the 1880s the sailor suit was a popular fashion trend for girls as well as boys, though one of the girls next to the tram appears to be wearing a gym slip or pinafore dress, which first appeared as school uniform around the beginning of the twentieth century. (Commercial postcard)

Lozells

The least well-documented BCT/CBT steam tram services were the two that had termini in Lozells, and to some extent, with a good deal of contradictory information, they are difficult to unravel.

The date that Birmingham Central Tramways Company opened its service to Lozells (Villa Cross) from the Old Square via Six Ways has been quoted as 1 November 1885. Since 1882 the Birmingham & Aston Tramways had had powers to build lines in Wheeler Street and Witton Road to permit a new route to Witton via Lozells and Six Ways Aston. The Birmingham Central Tramways refused to allow Aston's steam trams on its future cable tracks in Snow Hill, as, although they were the same gauge and it was theoretically possible to operate both modes of transport on the same track, BCT considered that a hot, leaking steam locomotive would eventually cause damage to the cable conduit or even the cable itself. The Birmingham & Aston Company built the line and then sold it to the Birmingham Central Tramways, which at first operated only a skeleton service, but a full service started on 25 October 1886. The route ran from the corner of Great Hampton Street and Great Hampton Row, along Wheeler Street, turning towards Six Ways, Aston, in Lozells Road.

In Lozells Road it met the inter-suburban service from Lozells to Lichfield Road via Six Ways, Witton Road and Church Road. A coke yard and small depot were provided off Witton Road nearly opposite Bevington Road. In addition, at Witton Square a short spur across Aston Lane to a point just short of Witton Railway Station was added at that time to enable BCT trams to reverse quite independently of Aston trams. The suburban Lozells–Lichfield Road service appears to have opened on 1 November 1885. The complexities of this operation are not clear once the steam trams got to Witton Square, but from the track layout it is assumed that it turned into Witton Lane and onto B&A tracks to work to the wrongly faced Church Road-Lichfield Road junction. Because of the track layout at Lichfield Road, in all probability a pilot engine would have to be employed. In this method a tram would arrive at the Church Lane-Lichfield Road junction and turn on to the out-of-town track. The subsequent manoeuvres with the arriving tram engine and the waiting pilot at the Church Lane junction all used the 'wrong-line' curves and obviously had to wait for the main-line B&A trams that were on their way out of town. After reversing with the trailer into Lichfield Road, the engines would swap ends, leaving the former pilot to take the tram back to Lozells with the former tram engine becoming the next pilot shunter for the arrival from Lozells. Once electrification took place in November 1904, the route was made much easier, as on arriving from Lozells the new electric trams simply crossed over Six Ways and took the direct route along Victoria Road to Lichfield Road. In addition there is an inspection report of October 1885 of a BCT line which left the Perry Barr route at Six Ways, Aston and turned into Lozells Road.

GREAT HAMPTON ROW JUNCTION

This is the junction on the Soho Road tram services, with Constitution Hill to the left of the large advertising hoarding and Livery Street to the right. The tram tracks to the left in front of the Rover 14 Sports Saloon are those in to Great Hampton Row. This line was built by the Birmingham & Aston Company but, because CBT would not agree to steam trams running over the cable tracks from the town centre and along Constitution Hill, CBT leased the line and only operated from inside Great Hampton Row; although there was a junction, it was only used for access. (H. B. Priestley)

BIRMINGHAM TRAM 524

On 1 April 1939, the last day of Corporation tramcar service, UEC-built tram 524 turns out of Wheeler Street on the 24 route and begins its journey to the Villa Cross terminus. The BCT steam tram service turned in the opposite direction and the overhead tram wires going straight on were used by the 5 route towards Six Ways, Aston. The two Lozells steam tram routes met at this point, so it was possible to almost get into Birmingham and also go to Aston Station, albeit by a somewhat circuitous route. (D. Clayton)

Villa Road

The terminus of the Lozells–Six Ways, Aston, and beyond steam tram service started at the distant public house at Villa Cross. The Villa Cross Tavern, built in 1879, not long before the steam tram service began, stood at the junction of Heathfield Road, Villa Road and Lozells Road. Steam tram photographs at this point are probably non-existent and so Birmingham tramcar 615 stands at roughly this former terminus with the Villa Cross Tavern hidden by the tram. Car 615 is working along Lozells Road when working on the 5 service in 1949.

Locomotive 2 in Villa Road (*Opposite below*)

Working on the Lozells service to Witton and Aston is Birmingham Central Tramways No. 2. This was the second of the first fourteen steam locomotives purchased in 1884 from Kitson of Leeds. This tram route was the only inter-suburban steam tram route in Birmingham. It opened on 1 November 1885 and went via Lozells Road before crossing the main-line route from the town centre to Parry Barr at Six Ways. The route was closed on 26 November 1904 and was converted by CBT to electric tramcar operation. Unusually the steam locomotive has a crew of two per driver, and standing at the end gate is a boy fireman.

BCT/CBT Route to Saltley

This route opened from Old Square to Nechells via Gosta Green on 29 March 1885, but closed by November of the same year when the Bloomsbury–Nechells section was closed, only to be surprisingly replaced by a horse tram service, which lasted until 31 December 1906. Meanwhile BCT opened their Old Square–Saltley via Gosta Green steam tram line on 24 November 1885; it closed on 31 December 1906 when all steam tram operations in the city were closed down after their lease to operate them expired.

SALTLEY TERMINUS

The steam tram terminus on the Saltley route was at the end of Saltley Road just short of Saltley Viaduct at the bottom of Nechells Place. Here there was a turning loop in front of the Carlton Theatre, which made the Old Square–Saltley route unique in Birmingham, as it had a turning loop at each end. The Carlton Theatre was opened on 16 July 1900 but was soon renamed the Coliseum and Gaiety. After 1921 it became a cinema until it closed in the early years of the Second World War. The Saltley route was linked in with the Perry Barr service, so that a tram starting at Perry Barr would go into Birmingham at its Old Square terminus before coming out of town via Gosta Green and proceeding to this terminus in Saltley Road. The whole process would be reversed, with the tram getting back to Perry Barr under two hours later. In the distance is the L&NWR railway bridge over Saltley Road linking Vauxhall station with Aston station. (D. Gladwin)

BCT/CBT Horse Tram Route to Nechells

This horse tram service was begun by BCT on 11 November 1884 and ran from Albert Street via Duddeston Row, Curzon Street to Vauxhall Road. After the steam tram service to Nechells was abandoned, the horse tram service replaced it along Bloomsbury Street on 24 November 1885; it crossed the Saltley steam tram line from Old Square before climbing the steep hill up Bloomsbury Street. After crossing Nechells Place the horse trams clip-clopped their way through the shopping centre in Nechells Park Road, passing Butlin Street where the two-road depot was located. After Butlin Street, the horse trams continued along Nechells Park Road before arriving at the terminus just short of Chattaway Street.

HORSE-DRAWN CARS

Fleet No.	Manufacturer	Type	Seating	Origin	Years
1–10	Falcon	Double-deck Open-top	20/18	BCT 1896	1884–1906
?	Various	Various		BTO	1876–1886

CBT Horse Tram in Albert Street

The town terminus for the BCT horse tram service was in Albert Street at the top of the hill near to the junction to Dale End. One of the Falcon open-top double-deckers has arrived from Nechells, and the horses have yet to be detached from the tram and taken round to the other end of the tram for the return journey to Nechells. The third horse would have been taken down the hill to Curzon Street where it would wait to assist the next tram back to the terminus. The tram is standing in front of a barber's shop where a shave would have cost 2*d*. (Birmingham Transport Gazette)

St Bartholomew's Church (*Opposite above*)

Passing St Bartholomew's Church and its tree-lined churchyard at the top of Duddeston Row is horse tram 4, built by Falcon of Loughborough for BCT in 1884. This road separated the churchyard from Park Street Gardens to the right of the tram. The knife board seating on the top deck could seat twenty passengers and seems to be better patronised than the lower saloon. St Bartholomew's Church was opened in 1749 to the designs of the architect brothers William and David Hiorne. It was built in a neoclassical Georgian style and was rectangular in plan. It was built in brick with stone dressings and had a small clock tower topped with a cupola over the main west door. The church had gabled ends with ornamental urns at each angle of the plain parapet, which can be seen on the roof. This area was, at the time, rather well-to-do, just to the east of the town centre, but with the opening of the railway to the nearby Curzon Street Station on 24 June 1838, the area rapidly changed from one of good-quality housing to one interspersed with warehouse and railway infrastructure. Despite this, St Bartholomew's became a parish church in 1847, but gradually lost its congregation and was closed in 1937. In 1942 the building was badly damaged by a German bomb and was demolished the following year.

DUDDESTON ROW JUNCTION

Another of the 1-10 Class of Falcon-built horse tram stands in Duddeston Row on the junction to the right, which took the inbound horse trams into Albert Street. Built in 1884 for BCT, they had long lives as they were not withdrawn until 31 December 1906. On the following day, Birmingham Corporation Tramways took over with electric trams. This route, once electrified and later numbered 7, was not financially successful and was replaced by trolleybuses on 27 November 1922, becoming the first route in Birmingham to be converted to this method of transport. The climb from Curzon Street is quite noticeable and explains why a third trace horse was required to assist the pair of horses. The driver and conductor pose for the cameraman in CBT days before embarking on the final climb to Albert Street. (Dudley Library)

The Junction Inn

Behind the uniformed tram drivers, the approaching Birmingham Central Tramways horse tram is travelling along Bloomsbury Street from Nechells in around 1890. Standing in the angle of Bloomsbury Street and Great Francis Street is The Junction public house, dating from the 1840s and unusually owned by William Butler's Brewery, based in Wolverhampton. Along Great Francis Street, later to be traversed by Corporation tram routes to both Alum Rock and Washwood Heath, are some already quite poor-quality back-to-back houses. Beyond this point the horse trams crossed Saltley Road before climbing up to Nechells Place and proceeding to the terminus in Nechells Park Road.

Nechells Park Road (*Opposite above*)

The CBT horse tram is standing in Nechells Park Road near to the Needham Street terminus in around 1906 sometime just prior to the abandonment in favour of the Corporation-owned electric trams. This section of the route only required a pair of horses to pull the Falcon-built tramcars. The company provided a service with a frequency of between six and eight minutes, which in combination with the small seating capacity of thirty-four passengers was quite adequate. Nechells Park Road was lined with mid-Victorian terraced houses, of which the better-quality housing was near to the horse tram terminus. The horse tram service stopped short of Chattaway where the steep hill in Nechells Park Road began leading into the valley of the River Rea.

HORSE TRAM 2

The horse tram service had replaced the short-lived steam trams, which only ran from 29 March 1885 until 23 November 1885. They were replaced by horse trams because the state of the track had deteriorated very rapidly, and with the poor loads being carried by the steam tram service it was decided that the poor track was not worth replacement but could cope with the much lighter horse trams. It survived until New Year's Eve 1906; this photograph, purporting to be the last horse tram, was actually taken three months earlier on 30 September 1906 in Nechells Park Road near to the turn into Butler Street. (Commercial postcard)

BCT/CBT Coventry Road, Small Heath

On 16 January 1886 BCT opened another new route to Small Heath. It started originally in John Bright Street before briefly moving into Hill Street later the same year. After 5 October 1886 the terminus finally settled in Station Street on the Midland Railway side of New Street station. The route left the town by way of Pershore Street, Bromsgrove Street and Moat Row, which it shared with the Stratford Road and Moseley Road steam tram services. At the Crown Public House in Bradford Street, the Small Heath route turned left into Rea Street and on reaching High Street, Deritend, turned right and proceeded into High Street, Bordesley. It then turned left beneath the Great Western Railway's bridge into Coventry Road. The steam trams went as far as Victoria Park, Small Heath, where the original terminus was reached at Dora Road. After just one year, a new coke yard was opened in September 1887 around 250 yards before the terminus, whereupon a new crossover was installed in order that trams could change tracks but also to gain entry into the coke yard. The CBT steam tram service was closed on 22 February 1905 when CBT electric trams took over the service using cars 181–188, which were very short-wheelbase bogie cars built by Brush. City of Birmingham Tramways Co. (CBT) electric cars ran from the steam tram terminus at Small Heath Park across the city boundary at Hay Mills to Church Road, South Yardley, from 29 March 1904, where a tram depot was built to house the new CBT tramcars. CBT had run a steam tram service from Birmingham City Centre to Small Heath Park from January 1886, but after reaching agreement with the Corporation, who re-laid the track, a complete electric CBT service ran between Yardley and Station Street from 23 February 1905. This state of service was to last only until the CBT leases expired on New Year's Eve 1906, after which the service was jointly worked with Birmingham Corporation. The joint CBT/Corporation electric tramcar operation on Coventry Road finished on 31 December 1911 and finally ended all CBT operations in Birmingham.

MOAT ROW NEAR BRADFORD STREET

In the twelfth century, Peter de Bermingham had a moated manor house which, though rebuilt, survived complete with moat, along Moat Row, till the end of the eighteenth century. For most of the nineteenth century, the old manor house site was used as an open market, which started in 1817 as a cattle market and later became a vegetable market. In 1881 the Smithfield Wholesale Fruit and Vegetable Market was built in Moat Lane on a site opposite the distant Alfred Woodward's canvas and bag premises. The site where the bustling open market is located was later the site of the 1903 extension to the Smithfield Wholesale Fruit and Vegetable Market. In the foreground, there is an elderly woman wearing a cloth hat who is serving a customer. What is a sobering thought is that she must have been born during the Napoleonic Wars in the early 1800s. The Falcon steam tram's double-deck trailer is No. 51, dating from 1885 and distinguishable by its seven-windowed lower saloon, and is on its way to Small Heath via Coventry Road. The Drovers' Arms, a converted late eighteenth-century house, has a large Mitchells & Butler's sign at the edge of the roof. Opposite the steam tram is the Birmingham Arms Public House, which was built in 1886 and was reputedly one of Birmingham's best 'gin palaces'. The road beyond the steam locomotive is Smithfield Street, which led to the distant Digbeth. This road had tramway tracks and was the only link between BCT's southern and northern routes via Meriden Street and over the horse tram service to Nechells. (Whybrow Collection)

BCT Steam Tram 65 and Trailer 54

Facing Birmingham in Coventry Road, Small Heath, is BCT steam tram 65. This was one of the thirteen Beyer Peacock 'Locomotive types' supplied by BCT 1886. The Beyer Peacock trams could always be distinguished by having an open tram body with a single central panel. The condensing apparatus was in the form of three radiator-style panels, rather than the Kitson style of what looked like round drainpipes. In 1893 all the Beyer Peacock steam trams were transferred to work the Small Heath route, thus dating this tram to being after that date and before the formation of CBT in 1896. Displaying the destination letter C for Coventry Road and Small Heath on the slip board, the trailer was built in Loughborough by Falcon in 1886 and is in its original condition.

CBT BEYER PEACOCK TRAM AND TRAILER 51

With staff and drivers posing alongside one of their charges, an unidentified Beyer Peacock steam locomotive. These were heavier than the Falcon and the Kitson locomotives, and rather too heavy for the trackwork. They relied on natural draughting and had to be nursed along in order to get the best results from them. The Falcon trailer is No. 51, built in 1885, with a seven side-windowed bogie tram that could seat a total of sixty passengers. The tram is standing in Coventry Road, near to the outer terminus in Small Heath in around 1897. The mustachioed gentleman on the right with a cap and a long coat does look like the late comedian and satirist Peter Cook's character E. L. Wisty – *just a thought!*

Coventry Road, Small Heath Terminus

On a warm summer's day in around 1903 an unidentified CBT steam tram travels along Coventry Road as it approaches Muntz Street on its way to the Small Heath terminus. It is outside Owen's large shop with the Co-Operative store next to it. The store was opened in 1901 and was the first purpose-built Co-Op shop in Birmingham. In the distance is the tower of Small Heath Baptist Chapel. The steam tram is one of the later six-windowed ones built by Falcon, which displaced the Beyer Peacock locomotives just before the end of the nineteenth century. It is noticeable that on the Coventry Road service, the steam trams seemed to operate more running chimney-first than, at least, the northern lines in Birmingham. Many photographs of steam trams in the nineteenth century reveal a slightly 'down-at-heel look' but this unit, sitting four-square on the track, looks nothing of the sort in its Corinthian green and deep cream livery, which in Victorian times would have received the detailed treatment of a craftsman painter at the CBT works at Kyotts Lake Road. (Commercial postcard)

Coventry Road c. 1904 (*Opposite above*)

The letter on the back of this postcard reads, '*This is the condition of Coventry Road at the present time and has been so for the last two months. If you ever visit us again you will not see the Traction Engines (steam trams) again.*' The workmen are laying wooden blocks to support the new electric tram tracks in the autumn of 1904. In the background is Victoria Park, while to the left the old steam tram tracks are still in situ and will remain so until the electric through service, jointly operated by the Corporation and CBT, is introduced. This would be some time away, because there are no traction poles in place to support the electric overhead, and the laying of new track was obviously an arduous and slow, labour-intensive job. (Commercial postcard)

STEAM TRAM 2

The driver of the last ceremonial Birmingham trolleybus on the evening of 30 June 1951, 90 (FOK 90), was Driver Frederick Leonard Gilks. He was sixty-two at the time and was allowed to take early retirement, as he considered himself too old to convert to being a bus driver. CBT Kitson steam locomotive No. 2 built in 1884 stands in Coventry Road, Small Heath, near to the coke yard, sometime before 23 February 1905 when steam tram operation ceased on Coventry Road. It has as its conductor, standing on the front platform step, one very young Fred Gilks, who despite his severe appearance was only around sixteen. The trailer is another of the many Falcon bogie double-deckers bought by Birmingham Central Tramways and inherited by City of Birmingham Tramways. (Whybrow Collection)

Coventry Road Coke Yard (*Opposite above*)

Standing in the entrance triangle to Coventry Road coke yard is a Beyer Peacock 'locomotive type' No. 66. There were thirteen of these trams that entered service with BCT in 1886 and by 1893 they were being mainly employed on the Coventry Road route. The coke yard was built slightly after the opening of the service, but the necessity to have depot premises on the route rather than the steam trams working directly from Kyotts Lake Road depot gradually became a necessity. As a result a small two-road depot was built later behind the Small Heath coke yard. The maintenance staff of the depot can easily be identified by their coke-stained overalls, while the platform staff look somewhat smarter. The depot closed on 31 December 1906. (K. Yerrington)

Coventry Road Depot 2012 (*Opposite below*)

Amazingly a few of the buildings that were built as part of the Coventry Road coke yard and depot, opposite Victoria Park, survive into the twenty-first century. Seen on 24 November 2012, between the late Victorian buildings on Coventry Road, the distant brick building through the yard was part of the car shed and just visible to the right is the coke yard office. (D. R. Harvey)

Tram 64 in Coventry Road Coke Yard (*Top*)

Standing alongside the brick-built coke bunker in Coventry Road coke yard is a well-polished tram locomotive 64. This Beyer Peacock locomotive of 1886 has the front destination slip board for SMALL HEATH, which was latterly rarely used on the locomotives as the trailers carried a similar side destination board as well as an illuminated route letter on the end shelter. These Beyer Peacock steam trams were very early production examples. The company constructed this batch of thirteen inside-cylinder engines for the Birmingham Central Tramways in 1886 with large-capacity three-tiered condensers. The wheels were 2 feet 7 inches in diameter with a 5-foot wheelbase. The overall length of the trams was 13 feet and the width 5½ feet. The cab was a very bare, steel-sheeted design, being completely open from the waist upwards, except for a short central panel each side. The roof was supported at each open end by two columns, and there was a half-door in each end.

CBT ELECTRIC TRAM 185

The Corporation constructed new electric tram tracks from Charles Road to the city boundary just under half a mile away under the terms of the CBT 1901 Parliamentary Act, and the electrified tram route was continued by the City of Birmingham Tramways Company as far as The Swan at Yardley. The company opened its electric tram service between Charles Road and Yardley in 29 March 1904 using new Brush-bodied electric trams 181–188. These were mounted on a pair of Brush 4-foot-long D-type bogies, but because of some unsatisfactory operation the eight trams were converted to run on Lycett & Conaty 8½-foot Radial trucks after 1905. One of these trams passes St Oswald's Road, which in 1904 was the penultimate easterly residential side road to have been completed opposite Victoria Park. Behind the tram is a CBT steam locomotive and trailer parked at the steam tram terminus. CBT began to operate its electric trams from 23 February 1905 as a through service from Station Street. After the CBT lease within the city expired on 31 December 1906, there was a joint CBT/BCT service from 1 January 1907, with the company supplying just eight trams with the balance of around forty being operated by the Corporation. When the city section of the lease expired, the Corporation took over the complete service on New Year's Day 1912.

CBT ELECTRIC TRAM 188

Standing at the impressive gates of Victoria Park is CBT car 188, which is still running on its original unsatisfactory bogies. With the steam tram track triangle entering the coke yard in the foreground, this was where the steam and electric trams met from 1904 until 1906. Victoria Park was on land given to Birmingham Corporation by Louisa Anne Ryland in 1876. This philanthropic lady also gave a donation of £6,000 towards the cost of landscaping the gardens. It was opened as Small Heath Park in 1879, but was renamed in honour of the Queen's Golden Jubilee eight years later! (Commercial postcard)

BCT/CBT Stratford Road Route

Unlike many of the BCT services, the Stratford Road route was fairly straightforward but did have the distinction of having the last steam tram extension in Birmingham. The BCT route originally terminated at the town end in Moat Row on 11 May 1885 and progressed up the steep hill in Bradford Street to Camp Hill. There it joined Stratford Road, Sparkbrook and passed Kyotts Lake Road, which was where the company works was located. The route then went past the junction at The Mermaid Hotel on the corner of Warwick Road, before climbing the steep hill up to St John's Road, Sparkhill, where the first terminus was located and where there was a coke yard. The inner terminus was altered by taking the route further into the town centre (though not desperately near!) to a stub terminus in Hill Street opposite the junction with Station Street on 20 June 1885. It was subsequently moved into Station Street on 5 October 1886. On 5 May 1899 the Stratford Road route was considerably extended at its outer end by around 1 mile from St John's Road to College Road, Springfield, just before the River Cole bridge. The route was closed when the lease expired on 31 December 1906. There was a briefly operated steam tram line built along Warwick Road to a point a few yards short of Greet Bridge. This was opened on 16 November 1887 and closed soon afterwards to be replaced by a horse bus service.

HILL STREET TO THE MERMAID

STATION STREET

The Stratford Road steam tram service started in Station Street after 6 October 1885, and the tram tracks can just be seen in the street on the right. The terminus of the Stratford Road services began in the shadow of the Midland Railway's side of New Street Station, which had been opened on 8 February 1885 by the extension into New Street of the Birmingham West Suburban Railway. This extension consisted of a train shed with two trussed arches, 58 feet wide by 620 feet long. The Stratford Road steam tram services began to start from here on 5 October 1886 when the Midland Railway's station was still virtually new.

TRAILER 29

Travelling along John Bright Street in 1886 is a one-year-old BCT Falcon-bodied 54-seater, six side-windowed, double-deck steam tram trailer. It was one of the 24–45 group of trailers and is being pulled by a Standard two-cylinder Kitson locomotive, probably No. 4, dating from 1884. Car 27 is working on the steam tram service to Sparkbrook during the only year that the Stratford Road steam trams operated in that central street named after John Bright (16 November 1811–27 March 1889), Quaker, supreme orator, Liberal MP for Birmingham from 1858, President of the Board of Trade and twice the Chancellor of the Exchequer. The tram is working inbound towards the U-turn into Hill Street. (Newman University)

STATION STREET (*Opposite above*)

After 1886, the BCT Stratford Road service ran up Hill Street and turned right into Station Street. By now in the ownership of the City of Birmingham Tramways, 41, a Falcon-bodied, fifty-four-seater, six side-windowed trailer, turns into Station Street and unloads in front of the Crown Hotel; the tall Shaftesbury Buildings are next, containing the offices of a variety of industrial and engineering consultants. Further down the impressively gas-lamp-lined street is the Market Hotel. The tram is displaying a side slip board for SPARKHILL and on the trailer's end screen is the destination letter S. The lack of any other vehicular traffic enabled passengers to unload at this small traffic island and then move further into Station Street, where kerbside loading was still a feature of the future. The trams would then turn right into Dudley Street and then into Pershore Street.

MOAT ROW

Travelling out of the town centre (it was not made a city until 1889) along Moat Row in around 1888 is Falcon trailer car 45. The steam tram is only going as far as Sparkbrook, thus being a shortworking of the service that normally terminated at St John's Road, Sparkhill. The two doors to the upper saloon at the top of the staircase are to enable passengers to get to both sides of the knife board seating. Although fitted with decency screens, there is no dash panel on the platform. The Georgian buildings on the far side of the road are getting towards the end of their lives and one of them has a notice stating, 'THIS LAND TO BE LET FOR BUILDING LEASE'. They would be replaced in the last decade of the nineteenth century. The coffee house on the right not also sells coffee but also tea and hot meat pies.

MOAT ROW AND BRADFORD STREET

A pair of steam trams pass each other at the Moat Row end of Bradford Street on 20 July 1901, just two days before the open market on the corner of Moat Lane was closed. The men appear to be haggling over the fate of the two horses and the foal. On the left is the Drovers' Arms at the corner between Bradford Street and Smithfield Street. On the right is the meat market and abattoir built between 1895 and 1897. The tracks in the foreground were only used to transfer trams to and from the northern and southern sides of the BCT system. (Birmingham CRL)

KITSON LOCOMOTIVE 36 (*Opposite above*)

Each one of BCT/CBT's tram depots had storage tanks for the acetylene gas that was used to light the interior lamps in the lower saloons of the passenger cars. Steam tram locos were frequently employed on 'works' journeys including taking gas-tank wagons to and from the depots. In April 1901, Kitson locomotive 36, built in 1885, was one of a pair of their Standard types supplied to the Birmingham Central Tramways Company. These short locomotives with their four-panel wooden coach-built bodies were only around 10 feet 11 inches long but could be driven from either end. It is turning from Smithfield Street into Bradford Street while towing two gas-tank wagons. Behind it is the Drovers' Arms, which not only sold ales and stouts but also provided breakfasts for the slaughtermen who worked in the abattoir on the other side of Bradford Street. (Tupenny Bros)

CAMP HILL (*Opposite below*)

Travelling out of Camp Hill and travelling towards the city centre is a CBT steam tram and double-decker trailer. In the distance are the twin spires of Holy Trinity Church, designed in the Georgian Perpendicular style by Francis Goodwin between 1820 and 1822. This area was not originally named Camp Hill but Kempe Hill, derived from a family name of the late fifteenth-century landowner. Camp Hill was probably renamed by association with Prince Rupert's camp here in 1643 during the Civil War. The shopping centre between Holy Trinity Church and the Ship Hotel dated from the 1840s and grew rapidly when the Midland Railway built their nearby goods yard. (Commercial postcard)

SHIP HOTEL, CAMP HILL

In the year before the CBT steam tram service was extended to College Road, Springfield, in 1899, an almost new Kitson 'Standard Improved' steam tram locomotive, No. 90, trundles towards the junction with Sandy Lane, on its way to the Sparkhill terminus, despite the destination board showing SPARKBROOK. When the area was developed after the opening of Camp Hill Goods Yard by the Birmingham & Gloucester Railway in 1841, the rebuilt Ship Hotel, which dated from around 1868, had a subtitled name which harked back to the English Civil War. This name was 'Prince Rupert's Headquarters – 1643', and they even had a statue of Prince Rupert in a niche below the Ship Hotel name. The pub was demolished in 1972 as part of a new road scheme for the area. (Whybrow Collection)

KYOTTS LAKE ROAD WORKS

Kyotts Lake Road Works was opened by the Birmingham Central Tramways Company in February 1885 as both an operating depot and a repair works, initially for steam trams and trailers and subsequently for cable and accumulator trams. Once electric trams had been introduced by the City of Birmingham Tramways in 1901, the works also built twenty-one new trams for its own use. The depot was off Stratford Road in Kyotts Lake Road between Port Hope Road on the left and the distant Grafton Road on the extreme right. Trams entered the works via the gates beneath the second large gable on the left. It was taken over by Birmingham Corporation Tramways Department on 1 January 1907 as a running shed for both the Coventry Road and Stratford Road routes; Kyotts Lake Road was closed as a depot and was converted to the Corporation's tramcar overhaul works in March 1908, finally closing in April 1954 after scrapping sixty-three trams which had been used on the Erdington routes by 6 August 1953, with car 597 being the last to be broken up.

CAMP HILL (*Opposite below*)

The panoramic view of Camp Hill shows the full extent of the area. Ravenhurst Street, forking to the left, was named after a large house in Highgate, a double-fronted building with Dutch gables which was in existence by 1748. Its long drive later became Ravenhurst Street. Sandy Lane to the right of the Ship Inn was plagued by the low railway bridge carrying the Great Western Railway's main line from Snow Hill to London and thus was never used by either double-decker trams or the later Corporation buses. A CBT horse bus working via Warwick Road from Acocks Green travels into the flat section at the top of Camp Hill, having climbed up the steep hill from Sparkbrook. Once through Camp Hill's shopping street it would come to an even steeper hill at the junction with Bradford Street. It is following a steam tram and trailer which is on the Stratford Road route and accordingly is carrying the route letter S on the end of the top deck end screen. (Birmingham CRL)

Kyotts Lake Road Works Paint Shop

The only parts of the old works to escape the fire of 9 February 2001 were the general stores on Kyotts Lake Road, the open yard behind it, the imposing wood mill, and the paint and body shop located alongside Grafton Road. The fire raged for four hours and it took ninety firefighters to control the flames. By September 2013 this was the only unaltered surviving building at the former works. They had to suck water from the nearby Grand Union Canal to tackle the flames destroying the building, which by this time was being used by a number of small furniture-manufacturing companies. This is the paint and body shop, and still retains the original high doors for the double-deck Corporation electric trams, which were some 15½ feet tall to the trolley plank, and is still being used as a metal-cutting workshop. The re-fronted building on the left is the former wood mill. (D. R. Harvey)

Loco 78 and Gas Wagon 3 (*Opposite above*)

Standing in the yard of Kyotts Lake Road Depot in around 1899 is Kitson Standard 'Improved' locomotive 78 with a four-panel coach built body, which was built in 1894. It is attached to CBT gas wagon 3, which was filled with acetylene gas, used for illuminating the passenger trailer cars. The works was a very large complex and this yard, almost hidden from the public, was accessed from a single entrance line in Kyotts Lake Road. (Tupenny Bros)

Locomotive 77 (*Opposite below*)

Standing in the central yard of Kyotts Lake Road Depot is Kitson Standard 'Improved' locomotive 77 dating from 1894. The men inside the tram are a driver and a fireman, although when in service the cab was the sole domain of the driver. Of the eight men posing at the side of the tram, there is a man with a shovel who would have been employed to load the coke onto the platform of the locomotive. In the middle is a smartly dressed conductor with his leather money bag and his conductor's badge. Of the four men on the right, the middle two appear to be works maintenance men while the gentleman with the waistcoat could be a foreman. On the right is a pipe-smoking man who is smartly dressed and appears to a manager. (Whitcombe Collection)

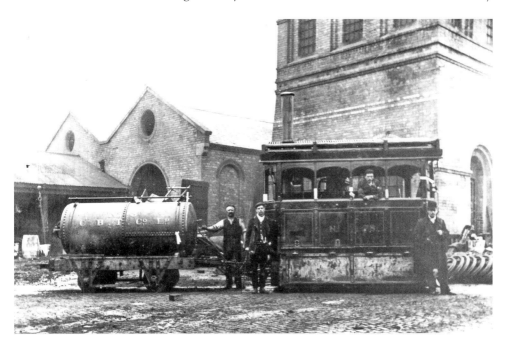

STRATFORD ROAD, SPARKBROOK (*Opposite above*)

Stratford Road in Sparkbrook was a thriving shopping area with a mixture of the small mid-Victorian buildings on the left and the larger, more imposing three-storey premises on the right. The BCT Company saw the Stratford Road route as a probable financial 'gold mine' and so it proved, as it always well patronised. The Kyotts Lake Road turn is on the extreme right where the tram works was located. In the distance is the Midland Railway's railway bridge carrying their Camp Hill line over Stratford Road. An outbound horse bus gallops on its way to Acocks Green via Warwick Road, using the tram track brick base as a better road surface on which to travel. Just look at the state of the road between the kerb and the tram tracks to appreciate why the horse bus is using the roadway that was maintained by the tram company! Behind it is a CBT steam tram on its way to St John's Road, Sparkhill. (Commercial postcard)

4651 (BX 54 XRM) (*Opposite below*)

On 2 September 2013, 4651 (BX 54 XRM), a National Express West Midlands bus, travels along Stratford Road, Sparkbrook, at roughly the same point as the horse bus in the previous photograph. The bus, a Volvo B7TL with a Wright H43/29F, dating from 2004, is passing the late Victorian buildings, although most of the original chimneys have been removed. The bus is working on the 6 route to Solihull via Sarehole Mill and Baldwins Lane. (D. R. Harvey)

STRATFORD ROAD, SPARKBROOK (*Top*)

Working into Birmingham along Stratford Road in Sparkbrook in around 1903 is a CBT steam tram and trailer in the crimson and pale cream livery, which was the last livery variation used by CBT on their steam trams. It is about to pass the newly completed Lloyds Bank on the corner of Braithwaite Street, and will shortly reach the Atkinson Brewery-owned Black Horse hostelry on the corner of Kyotts Lake Road, which had been built in 1880, which for many years was an important landmark in Sparkbrook. On the left is Main Street, which was one of the side roads that led to Moseley Road in Balsall Heath. (Commercial postcard)

STRATFORD ROAD AT FARM ROAD

There was frantic activity on the surviving CBT steam tram routes as, with the leases about to expire on 31 December 1906, there was a requirement for a seamless change to the Corporation's new electric tram service. This work was begun in the early autumn of 1906, relegating the soon-to-be-replaced steam trams to single-line working around the new trackwork excavations for the new electric tramway track. The navvies are working hard on this section of Stratford Road at the junction with Farm Road, as the Falcon steam tram moves off towards Camp Hill. The steam loco is emitting smoke from its chimney, to which the authorities frequently turned a blind eye in the last few months of CBT steam tram operation. (Whybrow Collection)

TRAILER 37

Trailer car 37 struggles through the snow in Stratford Road on New Year's Eve 1906, the last day of steam tram operation. It is travelling towards the city and has just passed Ladypool Road. The wires for the electric trams can be seen overhead, in readiness for the replacement. The car is a fifty-four-seat bogie car built in 1885 and has a canopy top with the unusual unglazed sides to the upper deck. The conductor is standing on the small balcony at the top of the rear staircase. This balcony was made necessary as the knife board seating in the upper saloon meant that there had to be access to both sides of the seating through two doors at each end of the trailer. To get to the top of the staircase there had to be a balcony so as to cross from one side of the top deck to the staircase. Only two hardy passengers are on the top deck while the lower saloon appears to be nearly full, as passengers huddle together to keep warm. Visible is the bell cord connection between car and engine.

TRAILER 132 (*Opposite below*)

The last steam tram trailers to enter service with CBT were six bogie cars, numbered 131–136, that were built by City of Birmingham Tramways at Kyotts Lake Road works in 1900. These large trailers had nine side windows in the lower saloon and were single-ended with only a staircase at the rear; they had seating for seventy passengers, with thirty-four passengers sitting on the upper deck on transverse garden seats. There were going to be four more trailers numbered 137–140 but with the impending end of CBT's operating rights at the end of 1906, it was decided to not to build any more steam tram trailers. Their problem was that they were bogie cars with the individual trucks mounted on the very end of the plate-frame chassis. This made them unsuitable for the costly rebuilding into electric trams that would later occur with the cable cars in Edinburgh. Trailer 132 is being hauled by an 1885 Falcon Scott Russell locomotive with a six-bay cab from the 37–50 series. The tram and trailer stand in Stratford Road outside the large house occupied by Lewis & Randall, the prolific Victorian photographic firm, on probably the last day of steam tram operation. The wires for the electric trams can be seen overhead, in readiness for the replacement. (Whybrow Collection)

LOCOMOTIVE 57 AND TRAILER 41

Falcon engine 57 and trailer 41 stand next to some wooden palings and beneath verdant trees when in BCT ownership. Unfortunately the location is not known but it could be on the Stratford Road route near Ladypool Road before the large Victorian villas were built. Loco 57 was the only Falcon two-cylinder compound engine, and entered service in 1886. The Falcon double-deck bogie trailer was a fifty-four-seater and dated from 1885. The loco is carrying the large letter S, which was replaced towards the end of the BCT operation. The reason for this posed photograph being taken is now 'lost in the mists of time' but it did involve the turning out of some of the BCT management.

STRATFORD ROAD/STONEY LANE

The view along Stratford Road from the tower of St Agatha's Church in around 1903 shows the steam tram tracks disappearing towards the Mermaid Public House at the junction with Warwick Road. On the right is the area around Stoney Lane. In the section of Stratford Road beyond the Baptist church built in 1879 on the corner of Palmerston Road is a CBT steam tram and trailer that is approaching the junction at Walford Road on its way to Sparkhill. By this date, Sparkbrook, although still in the Parish of Yardley UDC, was virtually complete as a suburb, with only a few side roads waiting for the construction of the then-normal tunnel-back housing. (Commercial postcard)

ANGEL INN (*Opposite below*)

A CBT steam tram travels towards Birmingham along Stratford Road in around 1903. It is approaching the Angel Inn. This public house was built in the eighteenth century as a coaching inn and was the last one on the Stratford Road before Birmingham. In the 1700s the road was little more than a dirt track lane, but after the First Turnpike Act in 1725, the first of the four main turnpike gates on the 21-mile road between Birmingham and Stratford was at the Ladypool Road junction, where a toll house was built next to the site of the Angel. It was this which encouraged travellers to become customers at the hostelry. The very prominent west tower of St Agatha's Parish Church is further along Stratford Road is in the distance beyond the steam tram. This impressive church was designed by W. H. Bidlake in a Gothic style but with Art and Crafts decorations. It is now a Grade 1 listed building. It is made of brick and decorated with stone, and building was started in October 1899. St Agatha's was funded by the sale of the site of Christ Church in New Street in the city centre after that church was demolished the same year to make way for shops and offices. Originally the font and one of the church's bells came from Christ Church. (Commercial postcard)

ORIGINAL MERMAID INN

Birmingham Central Tramways opened its route along Stratford Road in Sparkhill on 11 May 1885 as far as St John's Road, passing the original Mermaid Inn at the junction with Warwick Road before climbing the quite steep hill to the terminus. The Stratford Road steam tram route was the fourth to operate along a main road out of Birmingham. A BCT Falcon-built double-deck bogie steam tram trailer, No. 35, built in 1885 as one of the 24–45 batch, is being pulled by a Kitson locomotive within a few months of the route opening and before the platform was fitted with a metal enclosing panel. It also has the very large route letter S in a style that was replaced around the time of the transition from BCT to CBT. On the left, waiting outside the Mermaid, is a horse bus working on the Warwick Road service. At this time the Mermaid was an important roadside inn, which had become a hostelry in 1751, though the Georgian facade of the building hid a property that predated the start of the Civil War. This still-elegant building was replaced in 1895 by the present Victorian building, which has had a chequered history but still survives at the time of writing.

MERMAID C. 1897 (*Opposite above*)

The Mermaid Hotel was barely two years old when CBT trailer 41, a Falcon double-deck six side-window bogie car dating from 1885, begins the slow slog up the steep hill in Stratford Road from 370 feet above sea level in Sparkbrook to 425 feet at the top of the hill. Coming down the hill is another steam tram on its way back to the city. The row of sixteen shops with the large gabled roofs between the Mermaid and Weatheroak Road dated from just after the rebuilding of the hotel, and this terrace seemed to attract a number of tailors.

MERMAID 1902 (*Opposite below*)

The rebuilt Mermaid opened in 1895 but the corner towers were destroyed by German bombs during the Second World War. As two teenage boys look quizzically at the photographer, a well-laden steam tram starts off up the steep hill towards Sparkhill in around 1902. It would then continue to College Road, Springfield, over the 1899 extension. In front of the Mermaid is a cabman's hut and a row of Hansoms in Warwick Road. The shops around this junction were at this time a thriving shopping area. Hansom Cabs were named after their inventor, one Joseph Aloysius Hansom (1803–1882), who was also the designer of Birmingham's Town Hall. The provision of a street bench and a pavement lined with still fairly young saplings suggests that this area between Sparkbrook and Sparkhill was very prosperous. (Birmingham CRL)

WARWICK ROAD

CBT HORSE BUS IN WARWICK ROAD

The steam trams operated by Birmingham Central Tramways first traversed Warwick Road on 16 November 1887 as a branch of the already well-established Stratford Road service. The service was plagued by poor trackwork and the inability to cross the River Cole in Greet because of the parlous state of the crossing point. As a result, the service was not a financial success, and closed after little more than a year's operation, reverting to BCT's horse buses once more. One of CBT's horse buses, No. 119, stands in the throat of Warwick Road opposite the Mermaid Hotel. It is working on the route to Acocks Green, using the original early nineteenth-century Greet Bridge. In the distance is the imposing Gothic-style tower and spire of the Wesleyan Methodist church on the corner of Medlicott Road, which would be destroyed in an air raid in November 1940. In later years one of the shops on the left would become well-known as the Mermaid fish and chip shop, a must for late-night cinemagoers emerging from the nearby Piccadilly Picture House. (Birmingham CRL)

WARWICK ROAD, GREET (*Opposite above*)

Warwick Road was always poorly photographed with large sections totally ignored. As a result there are very few trams or buses captured on film travelling between Stratford Road and Acocks Green. About halfway along the steam tram route to Greet Bridge was the very narrow section between Mountford Street on the right and Percy Road in the distance opposite the Wagon & Horses Public House. The road was briefly traversed by the BCT steam tram service for a few months beginning in 1887, but then it reverted to horse buses. Birmingham Corporation began their tram service on 2 February 1916, initially as far as Broad Road, Acocks Green. This section was the only one in Birmingham that had traffic lights at either end in order to control the passage of the tramcars. The narrow road running through Greet's shopping centre lacks the traction poles and tram tracks on this postcard, which was posted on 17 June 1913. (Commercial postcard)

GREET BRIDGE, WARWICK ROAD

The terminus of the BCT steam tram service was just short of the original River Cole Bridge, which was considered to be too fragile to carry these heavy vehicles. Yardley Rural District Council replaced the bridge in 1902 but this was some fourteen years after the last steam trams had operated. On 24 November 2012, the bridge was substantially unaltered some 110 years after it had been constructed. (D. Harvey)

SPARKHILL TO SPRINGFIELD

STRATFORD ROAD, SPARKHILL

Two City of Birmingham Tramway steam trams and their trailers pass each other opposite the St John's Road coke depot in around 1900. This was the location of the original terminus of the Stratford Road steam tram service before it was extended to College Road, Springfield, in May 1899. This area of Sparkhill was built in the 1890s and so was still a new development when the route was lengthened by around 1 mile. It had an extensive shopping centre and was soon attracting more shoppers than the nearby Sparkbrook, which lay at the bottom of the hill beyond the two trams. The entrance to the depot is adjacent to the low building alongside the gas lamp on the left. (Commercial postcard)

ST JOHN'S ROAD COKE YARD (*Opposite above*)

The St John's Road coke yard was actually in Stratford Road and was used to replenish the steam trams with both coke and water. Perhaps such yards should have been water yards. Having been replenished, CBT loco 27, a Falcon-built tram dating from 1885, originally constructed as a four-cylinder compound, waits to pull its trailer out into Stratford Road. Tram 27 was later rebuilt as a Standard two-cylinder locomotive, becoming identical to the following 28–34 batch. The trailer is car 48, also constructed by the Falcon Company as one of their 1885 double-decker canopy-top bogie cars. These sat thirty passengers in each saloon and had seven, glazed lower-saloon side windows.

SALVATION ARMY CITADEL, STRATFORD ROAD (*Opposite below*)

After the CBT's steam tram service was closed on 31 December 1906, all locomotives, trailers and moveable infrastructure had to be removed. The coke yard site in Sparkhill was quickly sold and purchased by the Salvation Army, who began building a citadel in 1908. The Citadel was registered for public worship in 1909, replacing the old one in Bard Street off the nearby Shakespeare Street. The 1890s shops on either side of the religious building reveal the true width of the coke yard, which had a pair of tram tracks in the yard that led to a single exit track with lines going on to both the inbound and outbound tracks in Stratford Road. Seen on 2 September 2013 it is now renamed by the Salvation Army as the Lighthouse Chapel International. (D. R. Harvey)

STRATFORD ROAD AT BAKER STREET

The weather at the end of December 1906 was pretty awful, with strong winds and snow falling every day after Christmas. During this period the work continued apace to prepare the steam tram routes owned by CBT for their conversion to electric power on 1 January 1907. In this week, the conversion crews were at work on Stratford Road opposite the junction with Baker Street. Two workmen are attending to the new overhead cables as they stand on the horse-drawn tower wagons whose worryingly wooden structures are fully extended. Behind the tower wagons on the right is the junction with Showell Green Lane. (Commercial postcard)

Sparkhill Library

The deep snowfalls in the last week of 1906 made the last operational days of steam tram operation in Birmingham very difficult. The regulations for making steam and smoke were largely forgotten, not only because by this time it didn't matter, but also because of the extreme cold making any sort of hot exhaust more noticeable. The Falcon tram engine is on its way from Springfield towards St John's Road on 31 December 1906. It is passing the junction with Court Road with, behind it, the Yardley District Council House. This was built in 1894, originally as the former Council House, and became Sparkhill Library in 1923. (Birmingham CRL)

Stratford Road at Baker Street (*Opposite below*)

A CBT steam tram hauling a Falcon-built trailer travels away from the Baker Street junction as it continues its outbound journey along Stratford Road towards the distant tower of Yardley District Council House and beyond that to Sparkhill Park. The tram has left behind the original Stratford Road terminus, thus dating this view to around 1902. Although the accoutrements of a working suburb are all in place, the lack of road traffic is noticeable, with only the single horse-drawn cart parked next to the Baker Street junction, although there is also a lone cyclist pedalling up the hill towards the tram. (Birmingham CRL)

STRATFORD ROAD

The only steam tram extension along Stratford Road was from St John's Road to College Road, Springfield, a distance of around a mile. This was opened on 5 May 1899 and was the last steam tram extension to open in Birmingham. Six bogie double-deckers, numbered 125–130, were bought from the Midland Railway Carriage & Wagon Company of Birmingham. These nine-windowed seventy-seaters were single-ended, a feature not seen again in the city until the motorbus age. An almost new MRCW trailer car, 128, is working on a city-bound S route and is about to meet an outbound steam tram and trailer. They are passing the Yardley UDC Council House located in Sparkhill near Court Road. It was built in 1894 in red brick and terracotta with a large tower, to the design of Arthur Harrison, and today serves as Sparkhill Library.

LOCOMOTIVE 45 AND TRAILER 131 (*Opposite above*)

Falcon engine 45 and CBT single-ended trailer 131 stand in Stratford Road's Springfield terminus near College Road, and this image clearly shows the chain used to link the tram and the trailer. The flag attached to the front of the locomotive is there to commemorate the last day of steam tram operation in Birmingham. Through the cab body can be seen the layout of the locomotive, with a tall stove pipe chimney above the smokebox and the elevated firebox at the rear. As this is the last day of the steam trams, minor damage had not been repaired; this included the unrepaired tear in the trailer's canvas roof above the knife board seating on the upper deck.

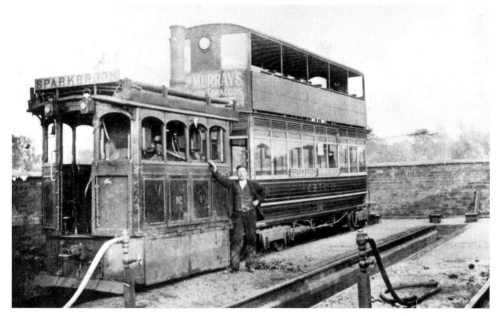

COLLEGE ROAD COKE YARD

Parked over the pits in the open yard at the side of the covered depot at College Road is ex-BCT Kitson locomotive No. 4 of 1884. It is towing trailer 136, one of the last CBT single-staircase, nine side-windowed, seventy-seater bogie cars that were built in 1900, and was only six years old when it was withdrawn. The method of constructing the side panels is clearly revealed as being of the wooden matchboard type. The depot was opened in 1899 and was known locally as 'The Field'. College Road was opposite Knowle Road on a reversing triangle just short of the terminus at the River Cole Bridge, which like its equivalent at Greet prevented steam tram operation on the southern side. It was transferred to Birmingham Corporation in 1907 and was used to store their withdrawn trams and those that were waiting to be rebuilt until the early 1920s. (J. Eades)

COLLEGE ROAD DEPOT SITE 2012

The entrance to the College Road CBT steam tram depot was opposite Knowle Road in Stratford Road, Springfield. The last CBT steam tram extension was to Stratford Road, Springfield, and opened on Friday 5 May 1899. By 24 November 2012 the location of the depot was well hidden and largely unknown. The entrance to the depot and the track within the yard ran parallel to the angled wall on the right. The boarded-up toilets occupied the space at the front of the open yard, which was reached by a single line that branched into three lines, each equipped with a maintenance pit. (D. R. Harvey)

BCT/CBT Moseley, Balsall Heath and Kings Heath

Birmingham Central Tramways opened their steam tramway to Moseley Village on 29 December 1884. This originally had its terminus at the junction in Bradford Street with Moat Row directly outside the Drovers' Arms Public House, but was soon extended along Bromsgrove Street and Hurst Street to terminate at the junction with Hill Street and Station Street on 20 June 1885. A new terminus was introduced later that year in Station Street but unusually in a dead-end beyond Dudley Street and almost opposite the back of the Market Hall in Worcester Street. With the demands of increasing traffic and congestion in this area on the western and southern side of New Street station, a further alteration was made to the Moseley route's terminus when it was first moved via the western side of Station Street to run up John Bright Street towards Navigation Street in 1886. This situation lasted for nearly fifteen years before the terminus was moved into Hill Street after 14 May 1901, with the trams coming directly up the hill from Hurst Street without deviating off this straight route. The new terminus was alongside the wall of New Street station just south of Queen's Drive and was the first tram route of any type in Birmingham to have kerbside loading. This was the final deviation, because once the new electric CBT tram service was extended into Navigation Street it went via John Bright Street away from the city and into Horse Fair, and this would have been against the flow of the incoming steam tram services. The Moseley Village route was given the letter M and ran to via Bradford Street, Moseley Road and Alcester Road to Moseley Village until 1904. After this date the Moseley Road route was extended to King's Heath along with the existing Balsall Heath service until closure on 31 December 1906.

The second CBT steam tram service along Alcester Road was the Balsall Heath line, initially to Moseley Village, which opened on 19 July 1886. This was extended from King's Heath on 1 February 1887 to Silver Street, where it terminated just beyond the steam tram depot. The route left the town by way of Hurst Street, Pershore Street and Sherlock Street. Having turned into Gooch Street, the route entered the Balsall Heath area, and on crossing Belgrave Road entered Longmore Street. In later days the next section of the route was giver the nickname 'The Chinese Railway' because it ran along interlinking roads taking different parallel routes in the Cox Street West, Mary Street, Edward Road and Norton Street section of Balsall Heath. Having crossed Edward Road, the steam trams crossed into Upper Mary Street and Park Road before joining the 'main line' at the junction of Moseley Road and Alcester Road. They then proceeded to Moseley Village and King's Heath.

LOCOMOTIVE 41

Falcon locomotive 41 and a seven-window trailer stand alongside the kerb next to the boundary wall of New Street station waiting to leave on the M service to Moseley after the route moved to the Hill Street terminus in 1901. The wall survived until 1964 when it was demolished as part of that year's redevelopment of the station. Behind the trailer are the gates to Queen's Drive, which ran between the L&NWR side of the station and the Midland Railway's later station.

MOSELEY ROAD AT HIGHGATE PARK (*Opposite above*)

On the last day of CBT operation on the Moseley Road route, an unidentified trailer travels along Moseley Road towards Bradford Street through the slush and mud. It is passing, on the left, Highgate Park and has just gone past Stratford Place. In 1875 the trustees of Elizabeth Hollier's charity wanted to develop her land for industry, but Birmingham Corporation bought it for a park. This was the first park actually created by the town council itself. It was the result of a desire to give some green breathing space to inner-city dwellers, whose lives were enclosed by buildings. The 14-acre Highgate Park was opened Joseph Chamberlain in 1876 to the designs of T. W. Coudrey on land that had formerly been a sheep and cattle fold for the Birmingham livestock markets.

MOSELEY ROAD (*Opposite below*)

The building of the Moseley Road library in 1895 honoured the promise Birmingham City Council had made to induce the residents to vote for amalgamation. Cossins & Peacock designed the building in terracotta and red brick in a freely interpreted Flemish Renaissance/ Arts and Crafts style. There is a prominent terracotta city coat of arms over the doorway beneath a tall clock tower, which was intentionally designed to be a local landmark. Internally the high-arcaded hall has a Beaux Arts plaster frieze in neoclassical style. This is a fine Victorian building and a fortunate survival of the extensive redevelopment of the district in the 1970s. The year is 1906, the last year of CBT steam tram operation, and one of their trams is travelling towards the city; the builders' scaffolding is already in place to aid in the construction of the public baths, which were opened in 1907 just after the steam trams had been withdrawn. (Commercial postcard)

MOSELEY ROAD

The emission of smoke or steam by steam locomotives in the street was forbidden by the Board of Trade but in certain circumstances it was inevitable and a blind eye was turned by the authorities. Falcon steam tram 53, built in 1885, is in Moseley Road just short of the junction with Park Road when working on the M service into the nearby Moseley Village when still owed by the Birmingham Central Tramways Company. The emission of steam, sulphur, smuts and smoke led to increasing hostility towards the otherwise highly efficient steam tram locomotive, which in all truth worked a minor, if unloved, miracle in the moving of people.

LOCOMOTIVE 38 (*Opposite above*)

City of Birmingham Tramways Falcon steam tram 38, built in 1885, with trailer climbs up the hill towards the junction with Park Road and the continuation of Moseley Road into Alcester Road on Service M to Moseley Village in 1906. The locomotive has its motion enclosed to meet the Board of Trade's safety requirements and prevent connecting rods from injuring pedestrians. The seven-bay, sixty-seat trailer was built by Falcon and weighed 3 tons 18 cwt unladen. It is carrying an advertisement for Priory Tea on the upper side decency panel. Priory Tea was a brand of Brooke Bond tea by the Manchester-based company that was started in 1869 when Arthur Brooke opened his first shop selling tea, coffee and sugar. (M. Rooum)

Trailer 56

Steaming up Alcester Road just after leaving Moseley Road is Falcon double-ended trailer 56, which dated from 1886. The bogie trailer car has a sixty-seat capacity, split equally between the decks, and is painted in the final CBT crimson livery. The garden seats in the upper saloon are being well patronised as the tram moves on its way to Moseley Village towards the Prince of Wales public house, which had been built in 1863, the year of the future Edward VII's marriage. Behind the garden walls, lying at an angle to the main road, is the early artisans' housing of the 1840s.

Diversions Through Balsall Heath

There are no known photographs of steam trams in the inner part of Balsall Heath on the section known as 'The Chinese Railway'. There was a shortworking lettered B which terminated at the junction of Longmore Street and Cox Street West. In order to get a feel for the area there are, substituted for steam trams, three post-Second World War views of Birmingham City Transport's 401 Class of open-balconied four-wheel trams in the area.

CAR 436

Services to Balsall Heath departed from the city centre through the congested streets off Sherlock Street and traversed particularly narrow Victorian-built streets, taking separate routes for inbound and outbound journeys. Locally, the specific pattern laid through Balsall Heath was disparagingly called 'The Chinese Railway'. Looking from Balsall Heath Road, an inbound Birmingham City Transport tram, 436, trundles from Cox Street West into Longmore Street when working on the 37 route from Cannon Hill. The curved track in the foreground is in Clevedon Street and was used by the outbound services. In steam tram days, trams in this part of Balsall Heath used Longmore Street in both directions and it was here that there was a designated shortworking, lettered B, which terminated at the junction of Longmore Street and Cox Street West. (F. Lloyd Jones)

CAR 416 IN MARY STREET

Looking rundown and shabby in the summer of 1949, inbound car 416 has descended Mary Street working on the 39 route and has stopped at the compulsory red stop before crossing Edward Road in the foreground. It is outside the Regency Dry Cleaners and barely gets a second glance from the three young women and the little boy in the pram. The opposite side of Mary Street, behind the photographer, was one of the earlier developments in Balsall Heath, with some small workshops and eleven houses being recorded in the 1841 census. Gradually the road and its associated buildings spread to the south up the hill towards Edgbaston Road and beyond to Park Road with the quality of the housing improving towards Moseley, becoming purely residential, and generally of two storeys. (R. T. Wilson)

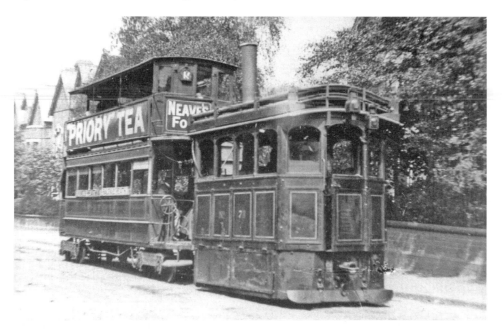

Loco 73 in Park Road

City of Birmingham Tramways' Kitson steam locomotive No. 73, built in 1894, is running firebox-first while towing one of the first series of Falcon canopy-topped, double-deck bogie trailers; built in 1884, it had knife board seating in the open-sided upper saloon. The trailer is displaying the route letter 'K', signifying that it is working on the Kings Heath via Balsall Heath route. This was opened in July 1886 by the Birmingham Central Tramways Company; the steam trams operated from Hill Street and their route was largely followed by the replacement Corporation electric trams that took over on 1 January 1907. Alternate journeys normally turned back at the Edward Road-Mary Street junction and would display the destination letter 'B'. On this sunny summer's day, around the turn of the twentieth century, the ensemble of loco and trailer stands in Park Road at the loop at Augusta Road. (M. Rooum)

Loco 26 (*Opposite above*)

Standing on the Balsall Heath route, possibly at the top end of Park Road is Kitson locomotive 26, the last of a batch of twelve purchased in 1885 by BCT. This tram had its locomotive parts well hidden by a four-windowed body, which normally concealed the inner workings and motion of the vehicle. Here the side cover had been lifted to reveal the heavy-duty connecting rods and the 0-4-0 wheel arrangement of the two-inside-cylinder locomotive. The mechanic also has the front side panel lifted up and appears to be ready to oil in the vicinity of the valve gear. The position of the driver reveals that these Kitson engines had their controls halfway down the side of the offset boiler and firebox making for a more universal driving position.

LOCO 77 AND TRAILER 55

Again very difficult to locate, but possibly just into Alcester Road and therefore facing Park Road when working on the Kings Heath via Balsall Heath service in early CBT days is locomotive 77, one of ten Kitson Standard 'Improved'. It was built as one of the last steam trams for Birmingham Central Tramways in 1896. It is pulling, firebox first, Falcon trailer 55, the first of the twenty delivered in 1886. This double-deck, seven side-window, canopy-top bogie car had a seating layout of thirty upstairs and thirty inside the lower saloon. The trailer has two staircases, and in accordance with Board of Trade Regulations a safety gate has been shut over the top of the platform steps.

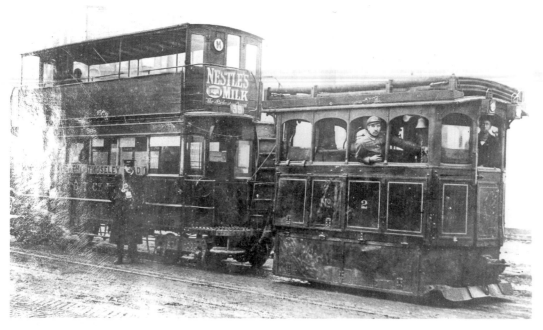

MOSELEY VILLAGE AND KINGS HEATH

LOCO 2 AND TRAILER 30

Not much of a clue here, either, except for the ghostly shape of a tall Victorian building. CBT loco 2, an 1884 Kitson engine, is pulling trailer car 30, a Falcon-built unit just one year younger than the tram. They are working on the M route to Moseley Village in the last few years of the CBT service as the trailer is in the last livery style. The CBT steam tram operation was not loved by the public because of the noise and pollution created by the locomotives, but at least they got a reliable and surprisingly long-lived service, with the passenger vehicles remaining well maintained until the end. (Commercial postcard)

at's Going on with the Vehicles?

ck run round some of the museum fleet that are not in service today..

e far end of the building, the Scammell Mechanical Horse now runs well, after servicing the engine, and the missing part of the cab structure has been replaced. The interior now needs tidying - it's a vehicle that gets attention when volunteer time allows!

Next, the Ford D-series tractor, OXS822M, has had most of the serious rust on its cab repaired and missing body-parts replaced and is once again available as a tow-vehicle inside the museum. Paintwork is still to be done.

he very early Transit, EEA508D, built in 1965, is now in running order, after repairs to the mechanical units and to the chassis structure; we hope it will venture out later this year for a test run. Next to the Transit, the A40 ice-cream van is ready for a partial repaint; like the Transit, it is now in running order and is booked to appear at an event on 6 September - will the deadline be met?

Ex-West Midlands Metrrider 685 still looks forlorn, lacking body panels, but work has been done; the wheels have been refurbished and the king-pin fault identified on its last MoT has been corrected. The panels were within a couple of days of arriving when one of the firms involved in supplying them went out of business, but hopefully that situation will soon be sorted.

In the Centenary Year of Guy, the Guy factory ambulance DDA70 has regained Guy green livery; it runs, though needing a rewound dynamo; with or without a dynamo, it should be ready for Guy events later in the year. Our other Guy, Arab LUF bus LJW336, may be running today; at the time of writing, the sagging front spring has been replaced and efforts are being made to get the bus ready to return to service.

At the back of the museum, newly arrived Optare Metrorider N155BOF is being readied for use; kindly donated by WM Police, it should serve as a promotional and sales vehicle at future events.

Work continues on the engine from the BMMO D9 6370; the cause of the problems has been identified, most parts sourced, and the block is now away at a specialist with the knowledge needed to use old engineering techniques..

Away from Shenstone Drive, Stratford Blue Leyland Leopard XNX136H and BMMO S17 5479 are both awaiting further attention, the Leopard for minor air system faults, though its front step area has been strengthened, while the S17 continues to mystify us with an intermittent fuel supply issue. Bristol VR 4714 is also off-site, but is in good health and is a victim of our limited accommodation for double-decks here at Shenstone Drive.

On their way…….

The 1954 Bedford Fire Engine is now expected at Shenstone Drive during July, where it will need a lot of work to bring it back to life, but with its 100 foot turntable ladder, it should be a crowd-puller!

Thanks to generous donations, these two former Harper Brothers Guy Arab coaches will return from Ireland in July, though not to Shenstone Drive at this stage.

To do justice to them…..

and all our other vehicles and exhibits, we need to raise some £50000 every year to pay for the building and to undertake the work we know you want us to do.

With your help, we can achieve it - donate, sponsor, become a member! Ask any of the volunteer staff for details

Moseley Village Loco 34 and Trailer 42

Birmingham Central Tramways opened their steam tramway to Moseley Village on 29 December 1884 and a few months later Falcon locomotive 34 of 1885 and brand new trailer 45 stand in St Mary's Row turning triangle outside the first Fighting Cocks Hotel, which was replaced some fourteen years later. The tram is in Alcester Road, Moseley Village, and is ready to return to Birmingham. The six side-window trailer is so new that it has yet to be fitted with decency screens along the sides of the top deck. As a result the central knife board seating can be seen.

MOSELEY VILLAGE

An unidentified steam tram and trailer leave Moseley Village after coming from Kings Heath on the K service. With St Mary's Row on the right, which was used as a left-hand turning triangle with Alcester Road, this image shows the junction with Salisbury Road, which was cut at the end of the 1890s through the Moseley Hall Estate and turned the village into a crossroads. Salisbury Road was named after the then Prime Minister, Lord Salisbury, the 3rd Marquess. He was three times the Prime Minister of the United Kingdom – from 1885 to 1886, 1886 to 1892 and 1895 to 1902 – adopting the policy of 'splendid isolation', keeping Great Britain out of European affairs and alliances, and was also the last British Prime Minister to serve from the Lords. He died in 1903, just about a year after the multi-gabled shopping block was built in Moseley Village. The tower on the right belongs to the splendid terracotta-detailed Fighting Cocks pub, built in 1899 at a cost of £4,000 by the Holt Brewery Company, together with the shops in St Mary's Row, also to the right; they were built with Dutch-style gables, and have a certain architectural panache about them, unlike the steeply gabled shops opposite. (Commercial postcard)

LOCO FROM THE 73-82 CLASS (*Opposite above*)

Travelling through Moseley Village on the K route to Kings Heath is one of the 73-82 Class of Kitson Standard 'Improved' locomotives that dated from 1894. The Fighting Cocks public house is on the extreme right with the single outbound track in the turning triangle in St Mary's Row alongside the pub. Although it is around 1904, there is only horse traffic in Alcester Road, as exemplified by the wagon on the right and the large pile of horse manure on the left in front of the row of hugely gabled early Edwardian shops. (Commercial postcard)

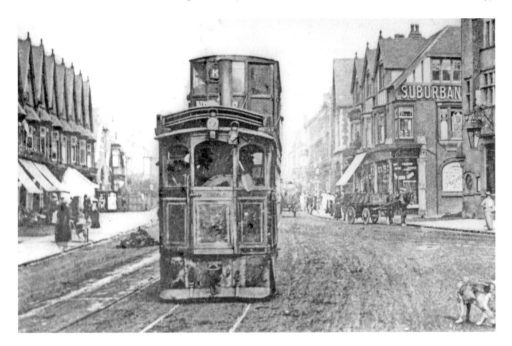

TRAILER 18

Passing through Moseley Village in 1902 on its way to Kings Heath, having worked from Hill Street in the city centre via Balsall Heath, is a City of Birmingham Tramways Company Falcon six-window trailer, 18, which by this time was around eighteen years old. To put this into context, a modern double-deck bus rarely reaches a service life this long! On this sunny day, passengers are boarding the tram via the rear platform and the staircase, while a smartly dressed woman carries a parasol as she crosses Alcester Road. In the background is St Mary's Row, with the fifteenth-century tower of St Mary's Parish Church showing above the rest of the surrounding buildings. (M. Rooum)

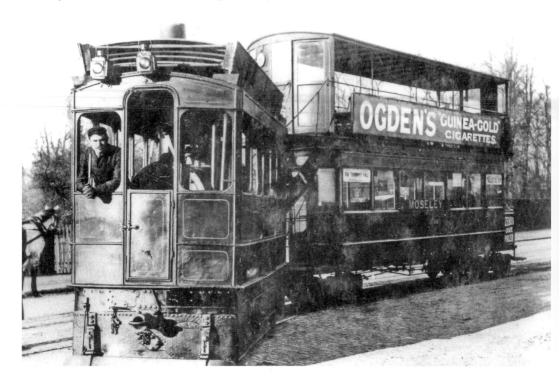

TRAILER 56 (*Opposite above*)

Turning into the triangle in St Mary's Row from Alcester Road in the middle of Moseley is a Falcon steam tram and Falcon seven side-window trailer car 56, built in 1886. The trams turned left and left again around a traffic island before drawing up outside the Fighting Cocks public house. The tram's various oil lamps are on the front of the vehicle while the condensing apparatus is prominent on the roof. The wooden fence in the background marks the boundary of the grounds of Moseley Hall, which would be given to the city by its owner, Richard Cadbury, in 1890 as a children's hospital; in 1899 its grounds would be cut in half by Salisbury Road, and open land behind the tram was used within a few years for the site of the distinctive gable-ended shops.

MOSELEY COKE YARD (*Opposite below*)

Just as the Stratford Road steam tram route had a coke yard at St John's Road, so the Moseley Road had a similar facility around 100 yards south of Moseley Village. A rather battered-looking Kitson steam tram from the 1884 batch that were numbered 1–20 by the BCT Company sits in the Moseley Road coke yard as it is replenished with water and coke, being manhandled by the lad with the wheelbarrow. There were two tracks over the pair of pits that led into a single exit line back onto Alcester Road, which could be reached from both the inbound and outbound tram lines. (W. W. Neal)

LOCO 61 (*Top*)

Standing near to the junction with Queensbridge Road, at the boundary between Moseley and King's Heath, is steam tram 61. This two-cylinder locomotive was built in 1886 by Beyer Peacock of Gorton as one of the 58-70 Class. The Beyer Peacock locomotives were an unusual choice for the various Birmingham steam tram operators, with only the South Staffordshire Company having trams manufactured by the company. The Beyer Peacocks could always be distinguished by having a completely open cab with the roof supported by a single central panel on each side. (C. Gilbert)

Loco 79

Standing in High Street, King's Heath, near to the terminus, is Kitson locomotive No. 79, which is hauling a Falcon trailer. On the platform of the trailer is the vertical wheel that operated the drum brake. The gate on the platform nearest to the loco is closed and the door to the lower saloon is locked shut so that passengers could only enter by the rear platform. The communication cord between car and engine is just visible. The tram has only a few hours of revenue life in front of it, as this is the last day of CBT steam tramway operation in Birmingham, with the overhead wires already in place for electric operation. The weather had been very poor at the end of December 1906 and the roadway is covered with slush. The trailer is carrying an advertisement for Brand's Beef Essence, which was similar to Bovril.

High Street, King's Heath (*Opposite above*)

The tower of the old Board School building dominates High Street, King's Heath. It was opened on 12 August 1878 on the corner of Institute Road. On the right is the King's Heath and Moseley Institute surrounded by iron railings. Standing on the single track with the terminus stub in the foreground is a CBT steam tram and trailer, which is about to travel towards the first passing loop at Heathfield Road, the next side road on the right after Institute Road, on its way to Moseley. The terminus of the King's Heath route was also where the depot was located. This was in Silver Street and the junction for the road is in the foreground on the left. (Commercial postcard)

Kings Heath Institute & Village

SILVER STREET

Standing in Silver Street with the depot behind it is Falcon Standard Scott Russell tram 40. These six-bay bodied trams concealed the smokebox and boiler but could scarcely hide the large firebox. This locomotive was built in 1885 and belonged to the 37–50 batch of trams built for the Birmingham Central Tramways Company, but by the time of this photograph is owned by City of Birmingham Tramways. The trailer is also of Falcon manufacture and it is about to run light to Moseley in order to pick up the M route to go on the direct Moseley Road route to Birmingham. As if to reinforce the use of the destination letter, the tram is carrying a board for MOSELEY.

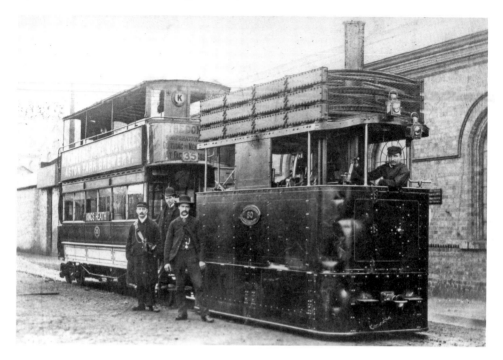

Silver Street Depot

Standing in the same location as the previous photograph in Silver Street depot's front yard is a Beyer Peacock 'Locomotive type' two-cylinder tram, but in the last years of the Birmingham Central Tramways Company. The tram is No. 60 and was built in 1886. However, this locomotive, one of the 58-70 Class, was withdrawn by CBT in 1898 along with trams Nos 61 and 62. All three trams were replaced in the same year by three Kitson Standard 'Improved' two-cylinder engines. The Falcon-built six-window bogie trailer is set up for use on the Kings Heath terminus.

Silver Street Depot with a Line-up of Trams and Trailers (*Opposite above*)

The four-road side of Silver Street steam tram depot is partly screened by a large group of visitors as well as depot staff. There is a Beyer Peacock steam tram on the second road from the left while the other three have just parked trailers in the shed. The two trailers on the right are both seven-bay Falcon cars, while the on the left is one of the early batch of Falcon cars with a flat-ended screen protecting the upper saloon. Although Silver Street steam tram depot closed on 1 January 1907, after which all the Moseley Road municipal electric services were operated by the brand-new Moseley Road depot, which had a maximum capacity of 90 trams. The changeover and movement of the CBT steam trams and trailers went very smoothly, with the trams being driven across Birmingham, from not just Silver Street depot but also from all the other depots. All of the steam trams due for scrapping went to Thomas Ward's scrapyard in Lea Brook Road, Wednesbury, save for one loco that burst its boiler at Silver Street and had to be abandoned there. Yet Silver Street depot was rewired and equipped with welded tram tracks so it could be reopened. This happened on 1 April 1908, but this would only be a temporary measure, as it was closed for the last time on 31 December 1912 after the Moseley Road premises were extended during 1912. (C. Gilbert)

SILVER STREET DEPOT

Part of the Silver Street steam tram depot in Kings Heath survives as factory shop. Although the roof has been re-clad and much of the brickwork refaced, the end wall behind the tree still has original brickwork. On 2 September 2013, the fabric of the car shed is in remarkably good condition, and perhaps it is a sobering thought that the depot last saw a tramcar of any sort over 100 years ago! (D. R. Harvey)

BIRMINGHAM & MIDLAND TRAMWAYS COMPANY

The Birmingham & Midland Tramways Company had a single route in Birmingham, which started from Summer Row on 6 July 1885 and closed when it was converted to electric traction on 20 November 1904. It was the line to Smethwick, Oldbury and Dudley, and left Birmingham by way of Sandpits, Spring Hill and Dudley Road to the boundary with Smethwick MBC at the Cape of Good Hope. The total mileage of this largely Black Country steam tram system was just under 11 miles.

PARCELS VAN 4

The electric trams' first terminus was at Summer Hill but there was a short extension into Lionel Street where they had a parcels office that was used by both the trams and the early motor buses. Being loaded from both the horse cart and the office is Van 4 in its chocolate-brown livery. It had a destination box that permanently showed PARCELS EXPRESS.

LOCO 13 (*Opposite below*)

Waiting outside the Cape of Good Hope in Dudley Road near to the Birmingham boundary with Smethwick and the famous M&B brewery, is steam tram 13. This was B&M's first Green-built Standard steam tram and entered service in 1885, before being rebuilt in 1899 by B&M using Kitson parts.

Birmingham & District 29

Standing in Edmund Street after the takeover of the Dudley Road tram service by Birmingham Corporation Tramways on 1 April 1928 is B&D electric car 29. This was built in 1904 and was also known as the 'Aston' type, as CBT built identical cars for their own fleet. This was one of the thirty-eight trams that operated on hire to the Corporation who were chronically short of trams at the time of the takeover. The B&D trams would remain on hire until the autumn of 1928 as they were waiting on the delivery of new trams (762–811) from Brush.

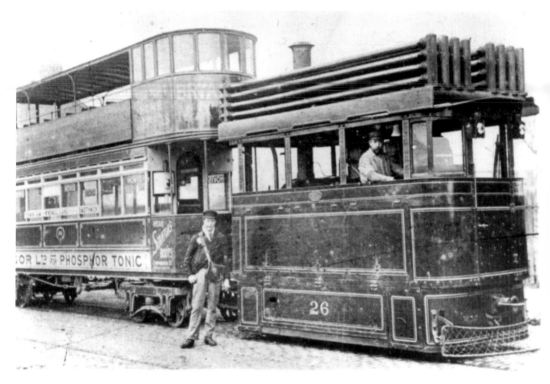

B&M STEAM LOCO 28 AND TRAILER 26

Locomotive No. 26 was one of four assembled by the Birmingham & Midland Company from Kitson parts, but with a bleak, noisy, iron cab and a modified version of the Burrell air condenser. Trailer 26 was also built by the company at their West Smethwick works and was single-ended, having a rear staircase and an extensive glazed screen at the tram end upstairs. It is at West Smethwick yard around 1900.

DRAWINGS

1. A side elevation plan of a Falcon steam tram locomotive shows the 0-4-0 wheel arrangement and the workings of the engine, including the valve gear, chimney, smokebox, boiler and firebox. The coach built six-windowed body is also shown.

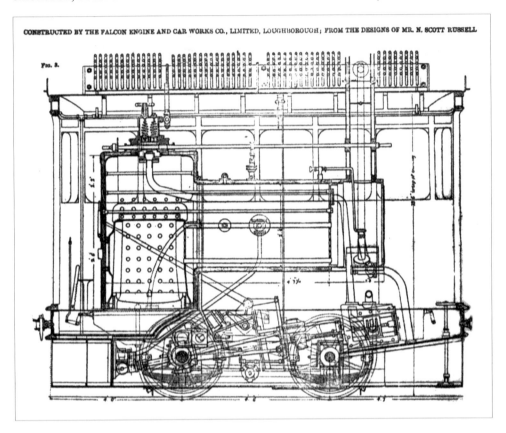

CONSTRUCTED BY THE FALCON ENGINE AND CAR WORKS CO., LIMITED, LOUGHBOROUGH; FROM THE DESIGNS OF MR. N. SCOTT RUSSELL

2. A set of working drawings of the layout of a seven-window Falcon bogie double-decker with garden seating on the upper deck, as supplied to BCT.

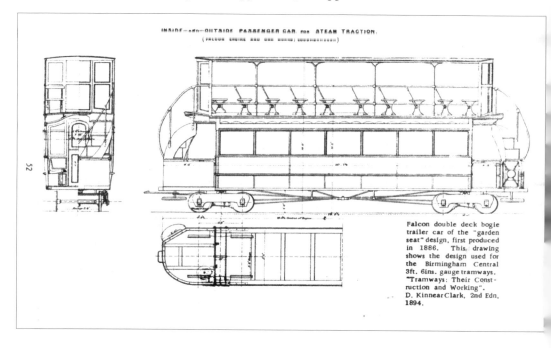

INSIDE and OUTSIDE PASSENGER CAR for STEAM TRACTION.
(FALCON ENGINE AND CAR WORKS, LOUGHBOROUGH)

52

Falcon double deck bogie trailer car of the "garden seat" design, first produced in 1886. This drawing shows the design used for the Birmingham Central 3ft. 6ins. gauge tramways. "Tramways: Their Construction and Working". D. Kinnear Clark, 2nd Edn. 1894.

REQUIEM FOR BIRMINGHAM'S STEAM TRAMS

A rather maudlin epitaph in the form of a poem to say farewell to the City of Birmingham Tramway's steam trams. This is rather ironic as they were not liked when they were running, yet nostalgically remembered at the time of their demise!

A Souvenir to be kept

In Loving Memory

OF THE

Old Steam Trams,

which succumbed to an Electric Shock. Dec. 31st, 1906.

1.

Though your breath it smelt like sulphur
And your sides were bare of paint
And you could'nt be called an ornament to the Street!
And oft our cash we've had to look for
Whilst some 14 stone conductor
Got the fares on top while standing on our feet!

2.

Though the rattle and the roar
As upon your way you "tore"
Made the houses all TO LET along the line!
Though your rocking made us bilious
And your lurching made us faint
And we thought that you would bust up any time!

3.

Still you had your points old Lumberer
For you took us all the way
We shall miss you, though we've hissed you it is true
Though rude boys oft called you "rotten"
You are gone, but not forgotten
Nevermore we'll gaze upon you but—
We'll never forget you.

P.S.

Do you ask me, O Departed?
How it was that though we smarted
And we grumbled—still we used you every day?
Don't crow, Steam Tram—you've no cause to,
Recollect that we were forced to,
Ride on you or WALK, O Lost One
For you were.............THE ONLY WAY.

SCOTT RUSSELL & CO., B'HAM, No. 129.

F.S.R.

REAR COVER IMAGE: ACCUMULATOR CAR 102

A passenger has just climbed the rear steps of car 102, which stands at the end of the tracks at the terminus of the CBT accumulator tramcar route at the junction of Suffolk Street and Navigation Street. The service to Bournbrook lasted nearly eleven years. This battery tram was built by the Falcon Company and had Elwell-Parker-designed series wound motors, running at 700 rpm and giving a maximum road speed of 8 mph. In front of A. Simpkiss's pawnbroker, and the CBT waiting room on the Navigation Street corner, is a recently erected traction pole for the new generation of electric trams to be introduced on 14 April 1901. Towering above these Georgian properties is the then recently constructed Birmingham Central Technical College opened on 13 December 1895 by the Duke of Devonshire. It later became the Matthew Boulton Technical College, but this elegant building was swept away in the 1960s when Suffolk Street Queensway was constructed as part of the Inner Ring Road scheme.